BELFAST

Edited by Carl Golder

First published in Great Britain in 2000 by
YOUNG WRITERS
Remus House,
Coltsfoot Drive,
Woodston,
Peterborough, PE2 9JX
Telephone (01733) 890066

All Rights Reserved

Copyright Contributors 2000

HB ISBN 0 75432 016 2
SB ISBN 0 75432 017 0

FOREWORD

This year, the Young Writers' Up, Up & Away competition proudly presents a showcase of the best poetic talent from over 70,000 up-and-coming writers nationwide.

Successful in continuing our aim of promoting writing and creativity in children, our regional anthologies give a vivid insight into the thoughts, emotions and experiences of today's younger generation, displaying their inventive writing in its originality.

The thought, effort, imagination and hard work put into each poem impressed us all and again the task of editing proved challenging due to the quality of entries received, but was nevertheless enjoyable. We hope you are as pleased as we are with the final selection and that you continue to enjoy *Up, Up & Away Belfast* for many years to come.

CONTENTS

Brooklands Primary School
    Craig Robinson   1
    Andrew Ferguson   1
    Lee Ferguson   2
    Lee McFadden   2
    Tammy Brown   3
    Rebekah Sachno   4
    Colin Spiers   4
    Jacqueline Fawcett   5
    Toni Clarke   6

Cairnshill Primary School
    Juliet Frimpong-Manso   6
    Lise Ross   7
    Ross Robertson   7
    Nadine Cargo   8
    Emma Leary   8
    Ashleigh Devlin   9
    Ryan Dickey   9
    Teri McConville   10
    Catherine Woods   10
    Steven Sparks   11
    Iain Chisholm   11
    Jordan Montgomery   12
    Natasha Jones   12
    Emma Prentice   13
    David Robinson   14
    Stephen Mullan   14
    Christopher Palmer   15

Carryduff Primary School
    Alan Fletcher   15
    Ashleigh Dobbin   16
    Jonathan Tripathy   16
    Edward Gregg   17
    Emma McClements   18

Julie Doake	18
Andrew Strain	19
Jonathan Payne	20
Susan McConnell	21
James Reid	22
David Pinkerton	23
Marissa Bole	24
Kirsty Kirkpatrick	25

Donegall Road Primary School

Matthew Bryans	25
Marie Shaw	26
Melissa Thompson	26
Michael Rea	26
Lynsay Smith	27
David McCracken	27

Edmund Rice Primary School

Fionnbarr McGovern	28
Ciaran Ferguson	28
Stephen Wylie	29
Paul McAuley	29
Fergal O'Donnell	30
Francis McCann	30
Peter Black	31
Christopher McGeough	31

Finaghy Primary School

Sam Davison	32
Takuya Inoue	32
Lynn Wallace	33
James Magill	33
Sarah-Jane Kinnear	33
Niall Thompson	34
Priyanka Nayar	34
Hannah Shaw	35
Caroline Claire Semple	36
Megan Ruth Connell	36

	Philip Moore	37
	Sara Uprichard	37
	Kerrie Boyd	38
	Scott McCormick	38
	Heather E Johnson	39
	Lucy Davison	39
	Zoe Prue	40
	Jordan Campbell	40
	Leah Thompson	41
	Christopher Dorman	41
	Joanne Ings	42
	Terri Boyd	42
	Mark Jordan	43
	Christopher Graham	43
	Erin McCracken	44
Holy Rosary Primary School		
	Annie O'Connor	44
	Fiona McGivern	44
	Niall Colton	45
	Ann-Veronica Campbell	45
	Oisín Quinn	46
	Conor MacGreevy	47
	Brendan Burns	47
	Anne Furey	48
	Laura Wilkinson	48
	Cheree Rock	48
	Richard Van Den Bos	49
	Matthew Whyte	49
	Ciaran McGowan	50
	Rebecca Hutchings	50
	Lauren Donnelly	51
	Christine Armstrong	51
	Kerri Faloon	52
Mercy Primary School		
	Nicola Edwards	52
	Sheila Farnan	53

Nadeen Trainor	53
Laura McEntee	54
Dymphna O'Connor	54
Ashleigh Maginess	55
Laura Murray	55
Christina O'Neill	56
Orla McLarnon	57
Nadia Whelan	57
Frances McLaughlin	58
Moya Weir	58
Sarah Cochrane	59
Sarah McGearty	59
Seanna O'Neill	60
Laura Captain	60
Stephanie George	61
Caitriona McSteen	62
Laura Hughes	62
Grainne McMullan	63
Stacey O'Hare	63
Sharlene Currie	64
Dominique McGoldrick	65
Sinead McKenna	65
Sarah Kane	66
Gemma Hamill	66
Gemma Grant	67
Natasha Butler	68
Vanessa Barnes	68
Francesca Glynn	69
Orla Carmichael	70
Danielle Finnegan	70
Katie Devlin	71
Emma Connolly	71
Kate Hennessey	72
Dawn Shannon	72
Eimhear Meehan	73
Maria Bannon	74
Fionnuala McGoldrick	74
Clare-Louise Wilkinson	75

Colleen McIvor	75
Emma McCallan	76
Maria Maginness	77
Joanne Rigby	77
Sarah McKibbin	78
Aoife Bradley	78
May Alexander	79
Nichola McBride	79
Rebecca Sheppard	80
Nuala Mary McAllister	80
Deana Thompson	81
Orlaigh McConnell	81
Lisa McAteer	82
Rachelle Ward	82
Caoimhe Britton	83
Caoimhe McGeough	83
Sarah O'Donnell	84
Emma Mowbray	84
Sara Madden	85
Nicola Williams	85
Léontia McGrann	86
Laura Fusco	86
Kelly Webb	87
Mariead McCann	87
Marcella Goudy	88
Grainne Gormley	89

Mersey Street Primary School

Danielle Quinn	89
Stephanie Bradley	90
Michael Jackson	91
Christopher Workman	91
Samuel Gray	92

Our Lady Of Lourdes School

Michaela Stewart	92
Frances Caldwell	93
Beth Mulhern	93

Aidan Small	94
Richard McIlroy	95
Fintan Maguire	95
Claire Leonard	96
Clare Geier	97
Mark McCloskey	98
James Parish	98
Claire Mulholland	99
Catriona Lawlor	100
Colum Joseph McCrudden	101
Eoghan Joseph Caldwell	101
Michael Casement	102

Rosetta Primary School

Matthew Spence	102
James Chew	103
Harriet Violet Cranston	103
Graham Richardson	104
James Bennett	104
Richard Burnett	105
Leanne Craig	106
Rebecca Gibson	106
Philip Todd	107
Peter Davison	107
Paul Dougan	108
Andrew McElroy	108
Dougal Crawford	109
Nicole Allen	109
Andrew Swain	110
Ruth Jennings	110
Daniel Stewart	111
Kathy Reid	111
Lesley Jordan	112
Rebecca Sleator	112
Jennifer Smyth	113

Karen Oliver	113
Sarah McKee	114
Thomas McGowan	114
Joe Shearer	115

St Anthony's Primary School
Shantelle O'Kane	115
Sami-Jo lavery	116
Gary Ferguson	116
Rory O'Hanlon	117
Seana Rooney	118

St Bride's Primary School
Orla Campbell	118
Maria Cushinan	119
Conor Heaney	120
Jeri Smith Cronin	120
Niamh Doyle	121
Orla Cassidy	121
Luke McCann	122
Ronan O'Kane	122
Rebecca Copeland	123
Aoife Campbell	123
Andrew Gribben	124
Maeve McGourty	124
Catherine Loughrey	125
Jamie Lavery	125
Hannah McKnight	126
Hannah McGrath	127
Carl Fitzpatrick	127
Conor McGuigan	128
Hannah Smyth	128
Ellen Toner	129

St Mary's Star Of The Sea, Primary School
Stephen Logan	129
Joanne Craven	130
Anthony Kelly	130

Mark Magee	131
Justin McReynolds	132
Deaglan Privilege	133
Mary-Anna Clarke	133
Ashlene Flynn	134
Ciara Rooney	135
Sinead McCourt	136
Shauna McAleenan	137
Shauna McGuiness	138
Stephanie Hall	138
Colleen McLaughlin	139
Matthew McIlveen	140
Paul O'Neill	140
Christopher Patterson	141
Kathryn Reynolds	141
Deborah Reynolds	142
Michael Kane	142
Kerrie O'Hanlon	142
Daniel Hughes	143
Gerard McLaughlin	143
Stephanie Murtagh	144
Eamonn Privilege	144

The Poems

IF I COULD UNDERSTAND

If I could know
Why space never ends
If I could understand
Why people have wars
If I could understand
Why people bully
If I were one of these people
I would understand

If I could understand
What it is like to be blind
If I could understand
What it is like to be deaf
I don't know
But someone else does.

Craig Robinson (11)
Brooklands Primary School

IF I HAD A MAGIC SHADOW

If I had a magic shadow,
darkening everything below,
turning it good and making it last,
while above, the shadow passed.

All the wars would cease,
so that we could live in peace,
if that went to plan,
maybe love would come to man.

Andrew Ferguson (10)
Brooklands Primary School

THE THREE MEN OF WINTER

There was an old man called Mr Noo,
He makes the sky white,
And he makes the air blue.

There was an old man called Mr Mo,
He comes by and leaves crystal snow,
He makes the world glitter,
And the air very bitter.

There was an old man called Mr Mush,
He comes and turns
The snow to slush,
No one likes him.

Everyone hates him,
We all wish
He would go away,
For many a day,
So we could play.

Lee Ferguson (9)
Brooklands Primary School

A WINTER SPARKLE

One day when I woke up
The ground was covered to the top
In the sky the clouds were gone
But left behind a shining glow.

But snow was still moving fast
The cars not moving a twitch at last
As still as the smoke floating past.

With bitter chills flying past
You feel like an ice cube running fast
People wrapped up in winter clothes
Them so warm and I so cold.

But at teatime the snow
Is slushy, wet and slimy too
And I'm sorry it is mushy.

Lee McFadden (8)
Brooklands Primary School

FALCON FLYING HIGH

I'm a falcon flying high
Above the shining sun
I take memories of the universe
And change them to be fun

I'll change sadness into laughter
And crime into peace
I'll change animals into people
And make the hunting cease

I'll turn darkness into light
And dead flowers into trees
And make the flowers' scent
Attract the honeybees

I'm a falcon flying high
Above the shining sun
I take memories of the universe
And change them to be fun.

Tammy Brown (11)
Brooklands Primary School

WINTER SWITCH

I woke up and it was dark,
I heard next door's dog bark.
Shrugging my shoulders I turned around,
Went back to bed not making a sound.
A witch came into my dreams and said,
'You shouldn't have gone back to bed.'
Then I was woken by a shout,
I looked out of the window
And this is what I saw.
A dog was making a print with his paw,
Then another shout
And children were running all about.
Toboggans, sleds, making angles in the snow,
How wet they will be, I don't know.
It did surprise me,
I think I will make a cup of tea.

Rebekah Sachno (8)
Brooklands Primary School

IF I COULD IMAGINE

Imagine what would be at the end of space.
Maybe a door leading to peace?
And you could have whatever you wanted.
Grab wishes and make them come true.
I would wish wars ended today,
Only maybe a punch here and there.
Now I hope my wish comes true.
Enemies will never be near you.

Colin Spiers (10)
Brooklands Primary School

WINTER DREAM

I open the icy door
And run outside
The beautiful sight
Just caught my amazed eyes

I blinked my big blue eyes
Once or twice
To my amazement
I saw a snowy sight

Bears, sheep, cows and ducks
Playing under the waterfalls
Donkeys, horses, monkeys and bugs
Playing in the deep grassy fields

I blinked again
Once or twice
Then I saw I was on my snowy lawn
Sitting on ice

The ice was as cold as water
Freezing up my red hands
I wonder if the animals were real
Do you?

Jacqueline Fawcett (10)
Brooklands Primary School

Snow

Everyone else asleep
Snow lying deep
Not a single peep
A tingle up my spine.

Sparkling snowflakes
Rivers turn to ice
Smooth and clean snow.

Snowmen dripping
Slushy, messy
Cold and dark
Rivers turned from ice
No longer nice.

Toni Clarke (8)
Brooklands Primary School

Winter And Summer

Heatwaves in summer,
Cold chills in winter.
Winter makes great effects with snow,
And hardly any days glow.
But if it gets too hot . . .
You might even scald!
Before winter comes,
Make sure that your fire is burning.
And before it gets too hot in summer,
Make sure your water is running.

Juliet Frimpong-Manso (10)
Cairnshill Primary School

A CLOWN'S LIFE

First they paint on you a smile,
(You think it's kind of fun for a while)
But then they bring out a stupid gown,
(The one that really makes you frown)
Then they give you a long red nose,
(It actually looks like a tiny hose)
Next they paint your face all white,
(Now you start to look all right)
Last they add a coloured wig,
(It makes you want to dance and jig)
Then they send you out on stage,
(You really are the total rage)
You start to tap, twist and twirl,
(Now you're dancing like a girl)
When it's over you're picked up by your wife,
(That's what it's like to have a clown's life!)

Lise Ross (10)
Cairnshill Primary School

CLOWNS CLOWNS CLOWNS

Clowns, clowns, clowns
Tall clowns and short clowns
Funny clowns and sad ones
Big shiny red noses and big floppy shoes
Baggy trousers and red curly hair
Clowns are good but sometimes bad
Laughter when happy and tears when sad

They juggle their balls up in the air
As custard pies fly everywhere
Clowns, clowns, wonderful clowns.

Ross Robertson (10)
Cairnshill Primary School

WINTER

When people go out to play in the snow,
My mum keeps saying 'No! No! No!'
And when I'm out, I build snowmen,
Remember now they're the *showmen*.

Houses into birthday cakes,
Veggies into rocks,
The grass turns into spiky hair
I wonder if you would care!

'Look at the clock it's time for bed,'
(I was so excited I bumped my head),
For tomorrow I'll be out to play: to twist and
Twirl and jump and curl.
In the winter snow!

Nadine Cargo (9)
Cairnshill Primary School

A FUNNY CLOWN

F   un is what a clown is made of,
U   nder the circus tent he plays around,
N   othing is too silly,
N   othing is too dumb,
Y   ou are not as dumb as he.

C   lowns, clowns, clowns,
L   oud as they can be,
O   ne throws a bucket of water,
W   hen the next falls over him.
N   ear that time a funny car came in,
S   oon they stampede all around.

Emma Leary (9)
Cairnshill Primary School

WINTER IS THE SEASON

Winter is the season,
where clouds are dark and grey.
Temperatures are freezing,
and fires are lit all day.

Good wishes in this season,
around the Christmas tree.
Children unwrap all their gifts,
and play so happily.

We need warm clothes in winter,
these are the winter ways.
With snow and frost and rain and fog
we look forward to brighter days.

Ashleigh Devlin (9)
Cairnshill Primary School

WINTER POEM

I look out from my window
The snow is falling down.
A blanket of white
Is covering the ground.
The children are playing,
Their snowballs fly about.
Their noise fills the air
You hear them scream and shout.
Winter is a cold time
There's frost and freezing rain
Go away quickly and bring the sun again.

Ryan Dickey (10)
Cairnshill Primary School

JACK FROST!

Lying in a blanket of snow,
Jack Frost with his horrible evil glow.
Watching all the children at night,
Making his teeth ready to *bite!*

Don't go to sleep, he'll get you then,
Watch out for his evil teeth again.
He'll bite anyone who is asleep,
I'm warning you now
Don't go to sleep!

He waits till it's cold,
Then gets ready to strike,
Biting fingers and toes alike.
He sneaks up to give you a fright
Watch out! Watch out!
Jack Frost is about!

Teri McConville (9)
Cairnshill Primary School

A SAD CLOWN

I saw a sad clown
In a dressing gown,
With red rosy slippers
With tears running down.

I saw a happy clown,
With a funny looking frown.
Dancing all around
Playing jokes down town.

Catherine Woods (9)
Cairnshill Primary School

As The Seasons Burn Out

As I sit in front of the fire . . .

I see spring and summer flying by,
And then on to autumn and winter.

Now all I see is snow and ice,
And trees are bare as can be!

As I sit in front of the fire,
I wait for spring to come.

I wait for lambs and ice-cream,
I wait for sunny days.

But all I see are flames,
So I'll have to wait

Until the flames burn out!

Steven Sparks (10)
Cairnshill Primary School

Autumn

Autumn means the end of summer,
The leaves are turning red and yellow.
Some are even brown and gold.
Days are shorter, nights are longer.
And it can be very cold.

Birds fly off to warmer countries.
Hedgehogs build their winter nests.
During this time I'm stuck inside,
Wishing that the winds would subside.

Iain Chisholm (9)
Cairnshill Primary School

SEASONS COME AND SEASONS GO

Seasons come and seasons go
Winter's harsh wind has to blow
Ice and frost sparkle and glow
Children are happy to play in the snow.

Spring comes dancing, full of hope,
Melting snow upon the slope.
Suddenly daffodils and snowdrops
Start to appear
The beautiful evenings become long and clear.

Summer is hot with glorious sunshine.
Building sandcastles oh so fine!
Sparkling water cooling you down,
Picking up seashells from the sand of golden brown.

Autumn leaves are falling, falling to the ground
Birds are flying off, warmer weather to be found,
Nights are quickly drawing in,
Street lights are not so dim.

Jordan Montgomery (10)
Cairnshill Primary School

A WINTER'S DAY

As I sit and look out of my window
At the beautiful frosty day
I see a pile of snow and wish
I could go out to play

I'd wrap up warm with gloves and scarves
And maybe even a hat
Then I'd run into my garden and
Scare my neighbour's cat

I'd stay out and play all day
Build a snowman with a carrot nose
Throw snowballs at my mum and dad
Until I can't feel my toes.

Natasha Jones (10)
Cairnshill Primary School

IN WINTER

The strong wind blowing outside,
The grass, roads and footpaths
covered in snow,
Icicles hanging from the trees and
the roofs of the houses,

But I'm inside keeping warm.

The car's frosted
The bitter cold air nips like a bird
Animals hibernating keeping warm,
The tree in the garden blowing
with the wind.

But I'm inside keeping warm.

Inside is warm and cosy,
A cat curled up beside the fire.
The smell of scones cooking
in the oven.
Inside there's no frost or wind
to freeze you.

I'm glad I'm inside - keeping warm.

Emma Prentice (10)
Cairnshill Primary School

WINTER IS COMING!

W   inter is crowding in on us
and it's getting very cold.
I   cicles are forming in the winter nights,
oh so cold!
N   ever go out in the cold night
because the frost will give you an awful fright.
T   rouble on the road
as cars slide uncontrollably everywhere.
E   yes of the public are so wide
looking for frost patches or even black ice.
R   ain is coming down now and the ice is melting fast -
at last the ice has gone!

David Robinson (9)
Cairnshill Primary School

WINTER!

Cold wind blows and
hurls itself around me,
The snow that falls is as
heavy as stones.

People say that winter is *terrible!*

I love to play in the
white, soft, delicate snow,
We especially like to make
those funny looking snowmen.

We say that winter is *brilliant!*

Stephen Mullan (10)
Cairnshill Primary School

WINTER

Winter is the god of seasons
Making people into snowmen
Turning houses into cakes
Making ice over the land

Now we are in the middle
Christmas is not too far
Santa is getting ready
And the children are waiting

Christopher Palmer (9)
Cairnshill Primary School

SHOPS

When I go into a shop looking for clothes
I see all the jackets hanging in rows.

I go to the shops looking for CDs
But then I wonder what happened to Louise?

When I go to the Mall I see lots of shoes on the wall
Then I wonder . . . What if they fall?

When I walk to Sainsbury's
I buy a couple of raspberries.

Later on I go to Gap
Where I buy a baseball cap.

After all that shopping,
I only have one thing to say
I'll never do that another day!

Alan Fletcher (11)
Carryduff Primary School

MY BEST FRIEND

When I'm feeling blue and start to cry
I always think of secret satin dry
the compact container the see-through lid
of any BO it will sure get rid
you're ready to roll in just two clicks
and it's guaranteed to be non-stick
the cold feel upon my skin is neat
no other deodorant can compete
I really adore that pleasant smell
about it everyone I have to tell
it's cool, it's fab, it fits in your bag
and I carry a picture of it from a mag
it's one of the things I most adore
and when it's finished I'll go buy more!

Ashleigh Dobbin (10)
Carryduff Primary School

BIRTHDAYS

Tomorrow is my birthday, I wonder what I will get
Maybe a dog or a cat - or maybe another pet.
Tomorrow is my birthday, I cannot get to sleep,
I am so happy I am about to weep.

I am so excited I cannot wait to see,
What my presents might just be.
I wonder what my parents are keeping
What are they wrapping up whilst I am sleeping?

In the morning I just cannot wait to see
If my present is a bike, a game or maybe a CD!
I am going to be eleven tomorrow
Oh, the thought of this makes you feel in heaven.

At last it is the month of my birthday - May
The thought of this makes me feel gay.
Soon it will be midnight when my birthday appears
I start to feel happy, then I start to cheer.

Today is my birthday, I wonder what I will get.
Maybe a cat or a dog, or maybe another pet.

Jonathan Tripathy (11)
Carryduff Primary School

DESTRUCTION DERBY

The speed, the style, the danger and fun,
the excitement and thrill that you get
from Destruction Derby.

The speed you get from your car
as you race round a corner and
thrash an opponent into the side wall.

The style as you speed along at over
100 mph in your beautiful car.

The danger when going around
a corner, an enemy tries to ram you
into a wall. Then you swerve and he
goes over into the wall instead.

The thrill as you leave the last
opponent in your dust.

Edward Gregg (10)
Carryduff Primary School

PETS

Rabbits like to dig and hop
With tiny noses and ears that flop
They live in hutches with lots of hay
They like to run and play

Dogs can be a very good pet
They do not like a visit to the vet
They like to go for a long walk
And one good thing - they do not talk

Cats like to run and play
And stay outside all day
Cats like to hunt for mice
There fur is soft and feels nice

Budgies are colourful and live in a cage
They can live until a very big age
They eat birdseed and drink a lot
They do not like to get hot.

Emma McClements (10)
Carryduff Primary School

THE SEA

The sea is like a roaring lioness
Hunting wild and free,
Her claws are the rustling pebbles
Beneath a wild and stormy sea.
As she hunts the day and night
I hear her roaring cry.
She pounces on and off the rocks
Hunting down her prey.

In the summer she is still,
As calm as she can be.
Lapping up the summer sun
Purring happily . . .
But when the winter comes, the sea
She's fierce and wild and free.

Julie Doake (10)
Carryduff Primary School

MY RABBIT

I have a rabbit
Snowy white
Everytime he sees the guinea pig
He always wants to fight

He walks and jumps
And digs holes too
Everytime he sees you
He wants to play with you

He plays in his hutch
Night and day
And everytime a cat comes
He runs away

He enjoys nibbling grass
And eats it very fast
When he eats it
He runs away fast

Andrew Strain (10)
Carryduff Primary School

SLEEPY GRANDA

Snore a-bye Granda
In your armchair
No one will wake you
No one will dare!

Under your newspaper
Worn like a wig
'Til we wake you at teatime
You can snore like a pig.

Granny would try to wake you
No one else would dare
As if we ever would
As you'd attack us like a bear!

When you eventually do wake
You are lifeless and lazy
You are a moan and a grump
And dull as a dead daisy.

After we have all had our tea
You go for a sleep once more
We all leave you to snore
As I shut the squeaking door
Night, night Granda!

Jonathan Payne (11)
Carryduff Primary School

CHOCOLATE!

Chocolate, chocolate,
What can I do?
I'd eat it for breakfast,
Lunch and dinner too!
So many favourites,
It's hard to decide,
Why can't you see?
It's keeping me alive.
Big sweets, small sweets,
Brown chocolate or white,
Just thinking about it
Keeps me up at night.
Mars bars, Crunchies,
Maltesers and all.
Left alone in a sweet shop,
I'd have a ball!
There is only one time,
When I scream and shout,
And that is when my
Pocket money runs out!

Susan McConnell (11)
Carryduff Primary School

MY CAT, FLASH!

I have a cool cat called Flash,
Because of the stripe down its head.
He always wants attention,
Even when I'm in bed!

Flash is very affectionate,
He'll always come when I call.
Except of course, when he's eating
Or chasing a bouncy ball.

He's black, with a white belly and feet
And big bright green eyes.
With a long slender black tail,
Oh, he's just as nice.

Flash loves hunting,
Even though he's never caught anything.
But he jumps on my feet under the duvet,
So at least, that keeps him in training.

Flash's best friend is one of our other cats - Tartan,
Who eats loads and loads of food.
But she really does not care
As long as the food's good.

I'd never give my cat Flash away
Not even for a money tree.
No matter what happens
Flash is staying with me!

James Reid (11)
Carryduff Primary School

DOCTORS

Doctors are people who help you to live
Of their expertise they are willing to give.
A baby may have the cold or the flu
You can be sure the doctor knows what to do.
If you feel sick or down in the dumps
The doctor will get rid of the grumps.

Surgeons will operate on you
With special instruments that give them a view
Of your organs and blood
Of which there is quite a flood.
They can transplant heart and lungs
Even remove your tongue!

If you find this rather gruesome
You'll find that there is a twosome:
Doctors and nurses pulling a trolley
Trying to look ever so jolly,
With scalpels, needles and knives
They're ready to save lives.

David Pinkerton (11)
Carryduff Primary School

OUR PETS

Gordy is my rabbit, he's very fluffy and white
He's very nice to cuddle, especially at night.
Sometimes he is naughty, sometimes he is good
He is very happy when he has had his food.

Goldy is a guinea pig and he's so small and brown
He climbs onto your shoulder then you have to take him down.
He may be cute and little, but he's certainly not dumb
'Cause when he's tired of playing, he will nip you on the thumb.

Patches, our other guinea pig is the biggest of the two,
He likes to run around the house and nibble at my shoe.
He is the leader of the pack but when the day is done,
He cuddles up to Goldy and greets him like a son.

Bobby is a goldfish and he swims around and round,
He used to have a friend, but he jumped onto the ground.
Bobby was so sad at this, he felt so all alone
Then mum went and bought him a new friend for his home.

Benita is a lovely fish she's mainly red and white
When Bobby swims after her she's never in a fright.
They've been the best of friends now for much more than a year
I think it's because our pets are happy living here!

Marissa Bole (11)
Carryduff Primary School

School

School is fun and good, some people don't like it.
We do games and work - like maths and English.
Outside, me and my friends play basketball.
Our maths is easy and fun to do.
Our English is fun but sometimes it is hard to do.
School is good and even my sister says so.
My friend Stephanie says school is fun too, like me.
The science experiments we do are very good.
My teacher Mr Smith, is nice to my class and me.
The Principle is nice and kind to the school
And the other teachers too.
I think my school is the best school in and world and
Has the nicest teachers as well.
My big sister Sharon goes to Newtownbreda and my
Big brother Jonathan goes to Inst.

Kirsty Kirkpatrick (10)
Carryduff Primary School

The Fairground

The fairground is coming
Oh, what fun we'll have.
Rides that go up and down,
Rides that go backwards and forwards.
Plenty of hotdogs and hamburgers,
Candyfloss so sweet and sticky.
By the time I go home
How sick I feel.

Matthew Bryans (11)
Donegall Road Primary School

GREEN

G orgeous
R ipe apples
E aten from the trees
E veryone loves them
N ice and crispy

Marie Shaw (11)
Donegall Road Primary School

A BAT

A bat has small wings
Has small hands
Goes out at night
To give people a fright
A bat has big ears to hear
People that make noises
In their houses.

Melissa Thompson (8)
Donegall Road Primary School

THE FAIRGROUND

I like the fairground
Specially at night
When everything's lit
And really bright
I love the rides
The thrills and spills
And I go home at night
And dream of the thrills

Michael Rea (10)
Donegall Road Primary School

THE FUNFAIR

When I arrived at the fair,
The sweet smell of candyfloss filled the air.
Everywhere I looked intense vibrant lights were flashing,
And I saw several kids on the dodgems clashing.
Screams of terror were heard from the ghost train,
As it entered into its scariest lane.
The big wheel was next -
The only place the people were able to relax.
In the coconut shy there were excellent prices,
Not to mention all shapes and sizes!
Our time at the fair has all run out,
But now you know what some of the rides in the fair are about!

Lynsay Smith (11)
Donegall Road Primary School

FAIRGROUND POEM

I love the Waltzers in the park
Especially when it's in the dark.
50p is a good deal
For six goes on the wheel.
On the Water Log you'll get wet
If you don't look out for the Water Jet.
You will squeal and scream in vain
When you see the ghosts on the Ghost Train.
The biggest in Europe is the Pepsi Max
But my worst fear is if it goes off the tracks.

David McCracken (10)
Donegall Road Primary School

BUGS AND SLUGS

Bugs and slugs you can find them anywhere,
Look in your school bag or even the stair.
You'll find them practically everywhere!
You can look in boats,
Look in drawers,
Look in places you normally ignore,
You can look in toasters,
Look in beds,
Or if you're hungry eat one instead!

Fionnbarr McGovern (11)
Edmund Rice Primary School

BEETLES

Beetles crawl under stones,
When you kill one you see it has no bones.
It always tries to squirm away,
When a bird is pecking at it all day.

They can walk upside down
You might say that's easy and frown.
They can do it without practising a lot,
Bet you couldn't do it in one shot!

Ciaran Ferguson (11)
Edmund Rice Primary School

An Autumn Poem

One windy autumn day
The leaves were swaying down the lane
They came to a wall so they had to delay
And a gust of wind was hitting the plane.

Up in Alexander Park
The tree - leaves turn rusty brown
They scatter on the ground
And the conkers are falling down.

I hold the rockets which are hot
In my hand they will burn
Out of my hand like a shot
All the way they twist and turn.

Stephen Wylie (11)
Edmund Rice Primary School

My Mum!

'Paul! Clean that.
Paul! Tidy your room.
Comb your hair
Wash your face
Brings us down the
Hoover.
Make your daddy a
Cup of tea.
Tell your brother to
Get down here. Now!'

Paul McAuley (11)
Edmund Rice Primary School

MY CHRISTMAS POEM

Christmas is coming
It's only round the bend
With presents to give
And cards to send.

It's a time for love
A time for joy
And Santa will be visiting
Every girl and boy.

Christmas trees are going up
Candy canes for all.
Just be careful that the tree
Doesn't break or fall.

Snow starts falling
Snowball fights all round
When I got hit
I started to frown.

Fergal O'Donnell (11)
Edmund Rice Primary School

WHAT MY MUM SAYS...

'Francis, Francis, clean your room
Francis, Francis make me tea.
Francis, Francis look at me.
Go to the shop to get a bap
Clean the dishes, mop the floor.
On your way out, close the door!'

Francis McCann (11)
Edmund Rice Primary School

PADDY THE WORM

I'm Paddy the worm
I'm long and firm
I wriggle from side to side
I slither and slide
To find somewhere to hide.

The hungry birds wait to catch me
But I'm nowhere to be found
I can hear them thud
Above the mud
For the minute I'm safe and sound.

Peter Black (11)
Edmund Rice Primary School

HALLOWE'EN

On Hallowe'en I will dress up
Like a cat or a bat.

I will around the neighbourhood.
Will it be a trick or treat?

I will eat some sweets
And some chocolate feet.

I will light a firework -
Swish! Look at it go to the moon!

Christopher McGeough (11)
Edmund Rice Primary School

KNITTING

My least favourite subject in school
Is knitting cos it's so uncool.
I'm really wick
It makes me sick
At it I'm such a fool.

Every Tuesday at ten past two
I've got to go to Miss Robinson's room.
It is so boring
I'd rather be snoring
Oh, will it be home time soon!

She asks for 20 stitches long
I'm so bad, I'll get it all wrong.
There are too many holes
Big enough for moles.
I can't wait 'til I hear the gong!

Sam Davison (11)
Finaghy Primary School

LEOPARDS

L eopards can hide in the leaves
E lephants are sometimes attacked by a leopard
O striches cannot run as fast as the leopard
P anther is a type of leopard
A nd hares are always attacked by leopards
R abbits are always attacked by leopards
D eers are eaten by leopards.

Takuya Inoue (9)
Finaghy Primary School

Boo!

What would happen if a cow said 'Boo!'
And what would happen if a ghost said 'Moo!'
If a violin went cluck
And a chicken went pluck!
What would happen if a rat said 'To wit to woo!'

Lynn Wallace (11)
Finaghy Primary School

Ouch!

Football, hockey, hate them all
I always get hit on the head with the ball!
One day I got hit in the side
It hurt so bad I almost cried.
This is a lesson to you all -
Don't get hit with the ball!

James Magill (11)
Finaghy Primary School

Teachers

I really hate some teachers
Sometimes they seem like preachers.
'Do this! Do that!'
Sometimes I feel like a welcome mat.
They are rotten creatures.

Sarah-Jane Kinnear (10)
Finaghy Primary School

My Favourite Animals

Sammy the snail
Leaves a silvery trail
One day in a gale
Some flew under my nail
And so Mr Snail
I feel very pale

Jimmy the bug
Had a head like a slug
He got stuck in a jug
So I gave him a tug
So wee Jimmy bug
Now owes me a hug

Micky the fly
Came down from the sky
He threw a big pie
Right into my eye
And so Mr Fly
I'm saying goodbye!

Niall Thompson (8)
Finaghy Primary School

Apollo 13

There is a rocket called Apollo 13
I watched it take off from the marine.
It took off with a blast
And went really fast
Up into the sky, so very high
And was never again seen.

Priyanka Nayar (11)
Finaghy Primary School

MONDAY MORNINGS

Monday mornings, they're all the same
and fortunately, there's no one to blame.
I always feel low, depressed and slumpy,
and sometimes I even feel a little grumpy.
Feeling down and very heavy
I dander slowly to school,
as friends call to each other, things like
'How do you do?'

As I entered the school grounds
my stomach rumbles,
'Whoops! I didn't have breakfast!'
I grumble.

                          I cheer up a bit
                          when I see my friends.
                          We always cheer up
                          at the sight of each other.

The nasty school bell rings
Oh, such depression that it brings.
Another school day, another school week.

                          Freezing and woozy
                          we crawl to our line
                          feeling as down as someone
                          who'd committed a crime.

As we enter the cloakroom
we always get squashed
and our school bags
drop from our hands.

Hannah Shaw (11)
Finaghy Primary School

THE SEA

Seaweed gathered all around
Dolphins and whales
And eels on the ground.
All types of fish with their beautiful scales
Dolphins and whales.

Firing cannons and stealing treasure
Pirates and ships.
Islands and maps.
X marks the spot - we're going to be rich,
Pirates and ships.

Dark caves and rocks
Seaweed and sand
Fish under docks
Friendly fish who shake your hand
Seaweed and sand.

Life in the sea is not so bad
With all the seaweed and all the sand.
Swimming and boating,
Finding crabs.
Life in the sea is not so bad.

Caroline Claire Semple (9)
Finaghy Primary School

MY FRIEND SYLVIA

Right now she's gobbling maggots
She loves insects - any type.
She smells like mouldy bread
And slurps water like a dog.

She speeds it down her slimy throat
While crunching black beetle bugs
And chases butterflies and slugs.
I like my pet Iguana.

Megan Ruth Connell (9)
Finaghy Primary School

ENVY

My envy is as green as a deadly weed
It tastes of horrible Brussels sprouts.
It smells of a burnt-out fire
It looks like a young girl falling and cutting her knee.
It sounds like the cry of a whale,
Its touch is as scary as seeing a ghost.

Philip Moore (11)
Finaghy Primary School

MONKEY

M   onkeys swinging
O   n leafy branches
N   oisy as can be
K   nowing they can play until the
E   nd of every day when
Y   oung monkeys fall asleep on their mother's knee.

Sara Uprichard (9)
Finaghy Primary School

ANIMALS

If I was a mouse I would stay away from the cat.
If I was a cheetah I'd be able to run really fast
If I was a cat I would look out for the mouse.
If I was a fish I would hide from the shark.
If I was an owl I'd be very wise.
If I was a giraffe I would reach up high in the sky.
If I was a whale I would gobble up all the fish
If I was a monkey I could climb all the trees.
If I was an elephant I could squirt water out of my trunk.
If I was a bird I could fly up in the sky.
If I was a worm I would squirm under the ground.
If I was a fly I would stay away from spider's webs.
If I was a dog I'd chase away the cat.
If I was a cow I could give you milk.
If I was a sheep I would give you wool.
If I was an angel I'd take care of you.

Kerrie Boyd (9)
Finaghy Primary School

STONE AGE

S   tone age people lived thousands of years ago
                                  man, woman, boy, girl, baby.
T   he stone age people used flints to scrape meat
                                  out of animals.
O   xen was part of the stone age diet
N   obody knows how stone age people learned to talk.
E   arly people could not make cheese on toast.

A   nybody could learn about the stone age
G   arments were made from animal skins
E   arly stone age people did not have Sky Digital - like us.

Scott McCormick (9)
Finaghy Primary School

THE RAINBOW

Rainbow, rainbow up so high
Reaching right across the sky,
All the colours really bright
Don't you think it's a marvellous sight?

Red and orange
Yellow and green,
Blue and purple's
A lovely thing.

God made the rainbow
That reaches across the sky,
God made a promise
To you and I.

This promise, the one I told you about
Is that never again
Will he send a flood.
I think it's great what he said to them.

Heather E Johnson (9)
Finaghy Primary School

VALENTINE'S DAY

Valentine's Day is awfully soppy
It would make you want to puke in the potty.
Oh dear, I've been sick on the floppy-eared bunny
And it is not very funny.
So now people think I am very loppy.

Lucy Davison (10)
Finaghy Primary School

Rain

Rain spoils a day
for everyone, especially me.
I look outside to another wet
and horrible day
I cry once more.

Rain spoils a day
for everyone, especially me.
I look outside to see
umbrellas and hoods up
I cry once more.

Rain spoils a day
for everyone, especially me.
I look outside the pictures
of puddles come alive.
I cry once more.

Zoe Prue (9
Finaghy Primary School

Racing Car

Racing car, racing car goes down the street
Racing car, racing car looks so neat
Racing car beeps its horn as it goes
It travels so fast to where nobody knows.

With its bright red body shining in the sun
The fat driver at the wheel is having great fun.
Tomorrow he has an important race, many other
drivers he has to face.
So racing car is put into the garage for the night
Everyone hopes that tomorrow will be just right.

Jordan Campbell (8)
Finaghy Primary School

MY BEST FRIEND

My best friend is good and kind
She always knows
When there is something on my mind.
She makes me feel I don't have a care
In the world.
When I am sad she cheers me up,
With a funny face
Or a great big hug.

She tells me all her secrets
And I tell her all mine.
Usually we get along quite fine
But sometimes we fight
Though we always make up,
Because you can't be without
Your best friend!

Leah Thompson (9)
Finaghy Primary School

HARVEST

H   for heather which in the fields grow
A   for apples in the trees glow
R   for roses lovely bright red
V   for vegetables by the watering can be fed
E   for elder flower from which the seeds fall
S   for sunflower so enormously tall
T   for turnips which do not flower

But God Almighty has all the great power.

Christopher Dorman (8)
Finaghy Primary School

The Visit

A special man came to our school today
From over the sea and far away
He was a TV superstar
A Gladiator by the name of Cobra.

He was very tall and very strong,
And all our school came along
To hear him talk about his TV show
And tell us everything we would like to know.

The next time I see his show on TV
It will bring back nice memories to me.
That was a very special day at school
The Gladiator Cobra was really cool.

Joanne Ings (9)
Finaghy Primary School

Dolphin

D   is for the danger that lurks under the sea
O   is for the other fish that swim along with me
L   is for the laughter that we all share
P   is for the people that come to visit me
H   is for the happiness that the people share with me
I   is for the intelligence that all dolphins have
N   is for the never-ending stories that are told about my friend and me.

Terri Boyd (10)
Finaghy Primary School

HIPPOPOTAMUS

H ippopotamuses only live in Africa.
I n water you can only see their heads.
P ygmy hippos weigh about 180 - 275kg (396 - 606lbs)
P ygmy hippos have oilier skin and can stay out of the water longer.
O ver the night hippos come out of the water and feed on grass.
P ygmy hippos are much smaller.
O f all land animals, only the elephant is bigger.
T hey spend most of their time in water and are good swimmers.
A frican hippos are the second largest land animals after elephants.
M ale hippos open their mouths to scare enemies.
U nder water they can stay for ten minutes.
S o that's what you need to know about hippos.

Mark Jordan (9)
Finaghy Primary School

THE SUN AND THE MOON

The sun -

The sun is big, round and yellow,
It shines brightly in the sky
Bringing sunlight to the Earth,
Just to make us smile.

The moon -

The moon is like a big lamp
Lighting up the sky so high.
The moon is a big star
With a big, happy smile.

Christopher Graham (8)
Finaghy Primary School

OSTRICH

O ut in the African bush
S wiftly I do run
T hey call me the flightless bird
R ight now they are chasing me
I have nowhere to hide
C an you help me find somewhere?
H ide my head? Yes I will bury it in the sand.

Erin McCracken (8)
Finaghy Primary School

FROGS

Fat, frumpy frogs
Sit on thick, brown logs.
By the ponds they sit,
Not moving a bit -
Along comes a fly,
In a flash, it's all mash.

Annie O'Connor (10)
Holy Rosary Primary School

SCHOOL

School can be fun,
Especially in the sun,
Playing chases with friends at break.
Sometimes when we come in,
We have an ache.
Instead of doing good work,
Sometimes we shirk.

Fiona McGivern
Holy Rosary Primary School

PEACE

Peace, peace, so far away,
Coming and going every day.
LVF, UVF, IRA.
Terrorists and arsonists please go away.
People who live only for death,
People who kill in one quick, subtle breath,
Just wanting to fight, fight and fight,
Oh What a terrible, heartbreaking sight!
Are we all exactly the same?
Do we breathe the same air, play the same game?

We can all live in peace and harmony,
Without the need for a terrorist army.
We can all in one small, subtle breath
Put an end to all this death.

Niall Colton (10)
Holy Rosary Primary School

MY MUM

I liked my mum,
She was very kind,
She even looked after
A person who was blind.
She liked me when
I was good or bad,
Then she passed away,
And I was very sad.
I still talk to her
Day and night as if
She was there every
Moment of my life.

Ann-Veronica Campbell (11)
Holy Rosary Primary School

THE GHOST

A ghost, a ghost! He came from behind,
He sent little shivers up my spine.

I turned around to see him but he'd disappeared,
He had gone behind me, just as I had feared!

Then suddenly there was a bright light,
It startled me, of course,
But what I saw was not a human,
It was a big, white horse!

It said, 'Hello'
I waved goodbye and ran and ran and ran
At the speed of light,
But there was no point - he just caught up with me,
A poor, old man.

I decided to ride him,
He took me up to the clouds,
To a bearded man with white robes
And a voice that was so loud.

I got off the horse and he disappeared,
And now forever I'll stay with the man with the beard!

Oisín Quinn (10)
Holy Rosary Primary School

THE WORLD

In the world there's happiness and joy,
Some happy children play with a toy.
Most adults go to work,
Some mental people go berserk.
A lot of animals make sound,
Baying like a bloodhound.
The world is not always at peace,
All wars should just cease.
A lot of people have religions on earth,
Some people would rather surf.
The world is not too bad,
I'm really, really glad.

Conor MacGreevy (10)
Holy Rosary Primary School

THE LIGHT

The light was in a shadowed tunnel,
Past the golden gate,
I saw a man behind me,
He said he was my mate.
But when I looked more closely,
As strange as it may be,
He had two golden horns
And a flaming red body.
So I walked up to the gateman
And sounded out in plea,
'Please may I come in Sir?
I'll be as good as I can be.'

Brendan Burns (10)
Holy Rosary Primary School

FRIENDS

F riends are brilliant to have.
R ight now I have quite a few.
I have a new friend, her name is Ann, like mine.
E very day I see my friends.
N ot everyone I know is friendly.
D on't be daft, make a few friends.
S ome people think to have a boy as a friend is weird.

Anne Furey (10)
Holy Rosary Primary School

OWLS

Owls are hunters, they fly at night,
They are never seen in daylight.
They are hunted down by the traps set,
There are barn owls kept as pets.
Owls have large eyes to hunt by night,
They are a beautiful sight.

Laura Wilkinson (10)
Holy Rosary Primary School

SUMMER

S ummertime is lots of fun, lots of fun for everyone.
U nder the trees in the shade is where I will be sitting.
M y family and I go on holiday and go to the beach for a paddle.
M y brother has water fights with me and my friends.
E very day is a long, warm day and the sunset looks lovely.
R eally, I love the summer. It is the best time of the year.

Cheree Rock (11)
Holy Rosary Primary School

MUSIC

Music is a wonderful thing,
The drum makes a bang and the triangle a ping.
Many different types like rock and rave,
And if you're not afraid to sing, you're very brave.
The electric guitar makes a loud, screeching noise,
The girls don't like that, only the boys.
Playing the drums is my favourite one,
If you try it, it's really fun.
Just take my advice and listen to the radio,
I'm sorry, but I need to go!

Richard Van Den Bos (10)
Holy Rosary Primary School

CROCODILE

C leverness is always the trick.
R evenge isn't always last.
O h my God, it's coming for us.
C ome on, we have to run fast.
O f course, it sees us as its food.
D avid's running slowly.
I 'll just run fast.
L et's see if it's coming for me.
E ven I don't know if I'm going to be tea.

Matthew Whyte (11)
Holy Rosary Primary School

FEAR

I was walking through the park,
It suddenly grew very dark.
At first, I thought it was a dream -
When I saw the banshee's silky gleam.
I ran all the way down an entry,
But then I noticed it wasn't empty!
Spiders were climbing up the walls,
Watched by the banshees with their gleaming shawls.
I turned and ran for my life,
That was when I saw the knife.
There was a man with deep, dark hair,
He killed me as I stood right there.

Ciaran McGowan (10)
Holy Rosary Primary School

CATS

Chasing after balls of wool,
Lapping up their milk,
Teasing dogs to come after them,
Sleeping softly on the chair,
Purring softly round my legs,
Scratching paintwork of the stair,
Miaowing for their dinner,
Wailing for a stroke.

Rebecca Hutchings (10)
Holy Rosary Primary School

WATER

We think water is everywhere,
But I know it's not.
We use it and we don't care,
It might not be there when we rot,
Because we waste quite a lot.
When we are watering plants with a hose,
Leaving taps running and
Having water fights too,
Also when you flush the loo -
Water is wasting because of you!

Lauren Donnelly (10)
Holy Rosary Primary School

LOVE

Red is the colour of love,
It could make you reach the stars above,
It reminds me of Italian pasta,
Very hot with pesto salsa.
Hearts can be broken,
But you can pretend
From a dream you have just woken.
Put friendship first,
Or your heart will burst.

Christine Armstrong (10)
Holy Rosary Primary School

FRIENDS

F riends are fun to have around,
R acing, chasing round and round,
I n and out of ice-cream shops,
E ating and licking lollipops,
N ow it's dark, let's go to bed,
D on't get mad, just rest your head,
S leep tight because tomorrow we'll do it
   all over again.

Kerri Faloon (10)
Holy Rosary Primary School

THE RIVER LAGAN

Trickling down the mountain side,
As fast as fast can be,
The River Lagan flows straight down,
Supplying water for you and me.

The river's getting slower now,
And wider as we speak,
Just like our grandparents,
Old, tired and weak.

Now the river's joined the sea,
Where we go paddling,
Where we get ice-cream,
Play games, shout and sing.

Nicola Edwards (10)
Mercy Primary School

LOOKING BACK

A flying contraption,
A motion picture screen
And a large clump of metal on wheels,
Electrical lights
And telephones,
A printing press, of course.
A camera that captures the image you hold,
Railway trains and cars,
Hot air balloons
And men on the moon.
Dinosaur bones were found.
You have to admit that it was
Quite an amazing millennium.

Sheila Farnan (10)
Mercy Primary School

A VIKING CHANT

Look out! Look out!
The Vikings are about,
With lashing swords
Going aboard.
They're going to Holy Island
To steal some hordes of gold,
Some young, some old,
It doesn't matter,
They are all fierce and bold.
Beware, beware,
You never know, they might,
They might be here tonight.

Nadeen Trainor (10)
Mercy Primary School

THE WITCHES' POT

At Hallowe'en fireworks go off.
Cats and dog have to stay in.
Doorbells ring all night.
People sing songs,
Children dress up,
Some dress up as witches.

Fireworks are colourful,
Fireworks are dangerous,
Fireworks going off make a bang.
Cats and dogs stay inside.
Everyone wants to hide.

Children dress up,
Sing songs at night.
Doorbells ringing all night,
Witches' costumes give you a fright.

Laura McEntee (9)
Mercy Primary School

MY NAME

D ymphna's my name, quite different I think,
Y et still I don't mind,
M akes me feel special,
P retty extraordinary.
H owever, I look
N ever just ordinary,
A nd perfect, that's me!

Dymphna O'Connor (10)
Mercy Primary School

ATTACK BY VIKINGS

The clashing of the waves as the boats pull in,
The sail waving, oars rowing, the Vikings' onslaught,
The bloodthirsty Vikings hurry out to kill.

Hurrying, scurrying, the monks try to get away,
Up the ladder into the round tower.
They look down horrified as the Vikings start to steal.

Wrecking and destroying the Vikings hurry in,
Killing and slaughtering everyone they can.
Oh! What a mess they make.

Their deed is done and now they run,
Leaving the monks lying dead,
All the treasures are gone.

Ashleigh Maginess (9)
Mercy Primary School

THE KINGFISHER

With metallic blue wings,
He swoops through the air.
Warm, chestnut-orange breast,
Such a brightly coloured bird,
Looks so dazzling at his best.

Darting swiftly everywhere,
Taking one big dive, he catches his prey.
Minnow, stickleback or eel,
He likes them all the same.
He eats, then preens his feathers,
For he is the kingfisher.

Laura Murray (10)
Mercy Primary School

VIKING ATTACK

Ruthless killings,
Slaughtering,
Oars pounding,
Birds screeching,
Terrorising the human race.
Preparing weapons,
Battle cries,
Bloodcurdling screams.
A swish of my axe,
A thud,
Heads roll.
The blood that stains my sword,
A sign of bravery.
Warriors with shields
And weapons.
Evil cries,
Terrifying my victims.
Families watch in horror
As I grab their loved ones.
Surrounding monasteries,
Valuable things taken,
Chalices, ornaments,
Whatever we can get.
Wherever we go,
We are dreaded,
We are *dreaded.*

Christina O'Neill (10)
Mercy Primary School

LONELINESS

Loneliness is being in hospital
Watching your parents leave the ward,
Thinking you've another twenty-four hours
Before you see them again.

Loneliness is moving house,
You have to make friends all over again,
Seeing different faces all around
And moving to a different school.

Loneliness can be caused by
A death in the family,
Watching the coffin being carried from
Their home to the church grounds.

Loneliness is not knowing anyone,
Being left out from a game,
Feeling frightened and unhappy.

Orla McLarnon (9)
Mercy Primary School

MY CANDLE

My little gold candle,
Shaped like a fairy ring,
It gives warmth and
Love to my room,
Glowing like a king's crown it burns.
The wax falls into a little pool of water,
Like tears dripping from my eyes.
I blow out my candle.
The wispy smoke creeps out of my room,
Quietly I watch it go.

Nadia Whelan (8)
Mercy Primary School

Autumn

Autumn is here,
Today is the beginning,
But the cease of summer,
The blazing summer days are over
And the colder days are here.

You can hear the farmers' harvesters,
Boy, they're loud.
The engines are harsh and tumultuous.

The nights are murky,
All nocturnal animals
Come out to hunt and feed.

The days are brief,
So off to bed early.
As we sit in our beds,
The nights are lonely and dull.

Frances McLaughlin (10)
Mercy Primary School

Sister

S ister, nobody can resist her.
I love her, nobody cannot love her.
S houting is what she loves to do best,
T roublesome, but she'll still beat the rest.
E ducated, she can count up to three,
R elaxing now he's in her bed you see.

Now, that's how I spell sister
And that's what it means to me.

Moya Weir (10)
Mercy Primary School

AUTUMN

The colours of autumn are coming!
Red, crimson, gold and brown,
Chestnut, copper and yellow,
The leaves are falling down.
Tumble, tumble, tumble down, down, down.
The town is covered with a street
Of gold, red and brown.

Autumn's full of colour, orange, red and brown,
While badgers, moles and rabbits are away underground,
Crunching, crunching, crunching.
What's that I hear you ask?
Jack Frost is dancing round far too fast.
Autumn days are here at last.

Sarah Cochrane (10)
Mercy Primary School

HORRORS TIME

H is for Hallowe'en
O h, look at the ghosts.
R is for rattling bones
R is for real witches,
O is for people being over-excited at Hallowe'en,
R is for running zombies,
S is for a spooky skeleton

T is for invisible teacher,
I is for inside a ghost,
M is for an ugly monster,
E is for everything that is spooky.

Sarah McGearty (10)
Mercy Primary School

VIKING ATTACK

Out come the Vikings,
They're going to attack,
Over to the monastery
To get their own back.

The roaring of the waves
As they launch their boat,
They can tackle anything,
Even wade through a moat.

When they reach the monasteries,
They plan to kill.
The war cries of the warriors,
They'll do what they will.

The panic of the monks
As there's hardly any time,
To grab their possessions
As the bells chime.

'Charge' the Vikings shout
As they run to the tower.
They grab their victims,
Because that's 'Viking Power.'

Seanna O'Neill (9)
Mercy Primary School

GOLDEN AUTUMN

Red hips peeping up,
Purple blackberry eating up,
Autumn leaves rustling about,
All the flowers with their big long stalks.

When, when, when, when will I see
A big, black and yellow bee?
When, when, when, when will I hear
The word 'autumn' right at my ear?

Laura Captain (10)
Mercy Primary School

THE WITCH

In a cave sat a witch,
She did not move, not even a twitch.
The cat miaowed and the owl hooted
And as you know, they both got booted.

Then she thought, 'Why don't I try
To make the handsome prince die?'
She couldn't work all alone,
So she dialled her brother on the phone.

Her brother was a demon wizard
And so they mixed some stew,
With nice young lizard
To make a magical brew.

One day the prince came by
And so they planned to make him die.
They put the potion in a cup
And so they turned him into a pup.

The witch got mad,
The wizard got madder
And so they both got
Badder and badder.

Stephanie George (11)
Mercy Primary School

VIKING ATTACK

Get out of my way or you will be a dead man.
As we row the boat through the crashing waves
Thinking of blood and dead men,
All the blood that stained my sword.
When you are fighting, you hear blood-curdling yells.

We warriors fight with no fear,
Men lying dead, their necks slit open.
Stabbing until it reaches the heart.

We will fight until we find precious gold treasure,
We will steal, we warriors have sharp weapons.

Hear the women crying over their husbands' bodies,
Kidnap monks and use them as slaves,
After that, we will be stinking rich!

Caitriona McSteen (10)
Mercy Primary School

THE JOURNEY TO WAR

The swirling waters slash against the boat of war
As the Vikings' solid arms swing the oars.
A sudden shout of 'land ahoy!'
As the monks and monasteries are in sight.
A heavy landing against the rocks,
Ready to attack home flocks.
Terrified monks crawl to safety
As the Vikings steal and invade.
The frightened monks wait till danger is over,
Notice that rooms are bare.
Their friends lay breathless on the floor,
While the Vikings leave the shore.

Laura Hughes (10)
Mercy Primary School

VIKING ATTACK

Out we go to sea,
Here we come, watch out.
We are the savage Vikings,
There will be blood everywhere,
They will be ruined,
Their lives will be miserable.

Will we survive?
Will we see our families again?
The waves are bashing, crashing,
But we are not afraid,
We will steal their precious gifts.
Here we come.
Watch out you monks,
We will burn your shelter.
Kill them! Stab them!
We will defeat them,
Their villages will be ruined,
Our tribe will not be defeated.
The Vikings!

Grainne McMullan (10)
Mercy Primary School

DOGS

Dogs
Cuddly, cute,
Jumping, pouncing, running,
I love all dogs,
Pets.

Stacey O'Hare (10)
Mercy Primary School

THE GYPSY

The gypsy, he is a very old man,
He has big ears and feet.
Everyone always stops to stare
When he wanders down the street.

My mummy thinks that he is quite sweet,
My daddy thinks he's small,
My sister thinks that he's generous,
But I don't like him at all.

His clothes are always dirty,
He never does his washing,
His hat has lots of holes in it
And his shoes are out of fashion.

His nose is big and pointy,
His beard is long and natty,
His hair is terrible, I have to say,
Because it's always tatty.

For breakfast he has burnt toast
With spaghetti hoops on top,
For supper he has chicken soup
With a buttered burger bap.

This very old man is very poor,
He has about 10p,
But where did he get the money for his stuff?
That's what's puzzling me!

Sharlene Currie (10)
Mercy Primary School

THE RIVER LAGAN

Up in Sleive Croob, there is a trickle of rain
That sounds like a gently played flute,
But as the trickle flows further, it gets louder,
So it is now like the clarinet that toots.

Now the Lagan is a small stream
Which has gurgled through the market town of Dromore,
Now watch the boats going up the canals,
Pulled by a horse, instead of rowed by an oar.

The Lagan itself now a river,
Dashes and dodges through the rocks
To Lisburn, famous for linen,
Then rushes off to Belfast Docks.

You can see and hear the shipbuilders,
And the chime of the Albert Clock,
Then we say farewell to the 'Lovely Lagan'
And hello to Belfast Lough.

Dominique McGoldrick (11)
Mercy Primary School

HALLOWE'EN NIGHT

W hile we trick or treat, all the witches are about,
I n and out of the full moon,
Z ombies are coming soon.
A fright will do no harm . . .
R eally spooky masks are going on,
D evils are running about on Hallowe'en night.

Sinead McKenna (9)
Mercy Primary School

The Kingfisher

His breast is warm, chestnut-orange,
His wings gleaming metallic blue
Or sometimes emerald green.
White for his cheek and throat,
His shining black beak catches his prey.

He spies a fish and darts,
His body is submerged,
Back he flies into sight
With water running off his back.
In a dazzling display,
He has caught his prey.

The river sparkles, glistens and gleams
And the weeping willow brushes it with her branches.
The river is still, until our friend is hungry again.

Sarah Kane (10)
Mercy Primary School

Stormy Seas

Across the raging waters,
Across the stormy sea,
You're cold, wet and dripping
At a tidal wave's mercy.

There's foam in the scuppers,
There's water up on deck,
It's really very slippery
And you're scared you'll break your neck.

You're really, really scared now,
There's dark rain clouds overhead,
Now that you're on this voyage,
You wish that you were dead.

Then you look out of a porthole,
You've reached your destiny,
You're there all in one piece,
It's been a scary trip, you see.

Gemma Hamill (8)
Mercy Primary School

THE KINGFISHER

Breast of chestnut-orange,
Wing of metallic blue,
The shine of emerald green,
His webbed feet of startling red,
A jewelled dagger for his tail,
Bright colours everywhere.

Swift and smooth he's in the air,
He darts to catch his prey.
He plunges towards clean water,
A swift, smooth pace.

He waits and watches patiently,
As he sits on the over-hanging branch.
His dagger-shaped eyes
Skim the cobalt blue river and brown reeds,
Hoping to see a stickleback.

Gemma Grant (10)
Mercy Primary School

KINGFISHER

Kingfisher, kingfisher,
My oh my,
What wonderful colours,
As you sit preening quietly,
Wings flutter gracefully,
As you swoop down for minnows.
Fishing greedily for your dinner
He dives down expertly,
In a flickering quiet world,
It soars high, it soars low
Fluttering, fluttering to the ground.
Colour of a dazzling metallic blue,
A warm chestnut orange.
Gets her nest ready for the nestlings.

Natasha Butler (9)
Mercy Primary School

MY BABY SISTER

I love my baby sister
Because she's very funny.
She loves her little teddy bear,
And also her bunny.
I love the way she eats her pies,
I hate the way she gets cross and cries.
When she's sad
I play with her,
Then she's happy,
And I'm so glad.

Vanessa Barnes (9)
Mercy Primary School

TERRORS OF THE SEA

Out at sea,
Out at sea,
Shouting, clashing,
rough, rough sea.
Rattling and squirming,
Clashing, flashing,
Seagulls circling.
'Yes, we're here,'
Cries someone out loud
As tall monasteries stand,
Ready for battle, here we go!
Run up the winding stairs,
Killing, stabbing, guts everywhere.
People calling us names
But we don't care.
Call us what you want,
But you will die!
Cutting off heads, slitting throats
And at the end we all run off
With our gold and silver
Jewels and gems,
Everything you could think of in the world.
Dead lie the Irish.
Ready for more?

Francesca Glynn (10)
Mercy Primary School

KINGFISHER

Metallic blue wings,
Chestnut-orange breast,
Fiery red feet,
A jewelled dagger is his head.
Feathers are emerald green, sometimes cobalt blue,
He swiftly swoops through the air,
Darting into the water to get his food.
He dives really fast,
Then hovers near the branch,
Then goes to dive for food
For the family to eat.

Orla Carmichael (10)
Mercy Primary School

THE KINGFISHER

The kingfisher waits patiently
Beside the stream
Near the reeds, long and green.
Its rusty orange breast,
Cobalt blue wings and fiery red feet
Help him make his beautiful nest.

Soaring gently through the air
Diving into the stream
To catch its food
Of fish and eel,
It's the most beautiful bird
That I've ever seen.

Danielle Finnegan (10)
Mercy Primary School

The Millennium

I had a millennium party,
I brought as many friends as I could,
To join in the fun and games,
To have as much fun as I would.

Having a lovely time,
Having lots of fun,
Eating lots of party food,
Mostly all the buns.

When the party was over,
I will never forget the day,
When I had a big party
And wanted the millennium to stay.

Katie Devlin (9)
Mercy Primary School

Viking Attack

On our way to Ireland,
Come on everybody, get those arms rowing
Or you will be very sorry,
I really mean that, ha, ha, ha.
I can't wait to smell that blood,
Those little fools screaming, ha, ha, ha.
We are evil,
Oh yes, thank you, what.
Get back to work now or I'll do the same to you,
No get back to work.
I really want them dead.
What? I told you to get back to work.

Emma Connolly (9)
Mercy Primary School

THE RIVER LAGAN

Along the River Lagan,
Where no one used to go,
Now new and fashionable,
To live where the river flows.

Starting at the river's source
It's as tiny as can be,
Let's start at the beginning
And see what we can see.

We are moving on rapidly
As the river grows and grows,
Houses and developments.
Students trying to row.

Passing Lagan Lookout
Where the water's nice and clean,
The water's getting strong now,
Funny how it used to be a little stream.

Arriving at my destination,
The Waterfront Hall,
Our journey's ended.
It's a journey to enthral!

Kate Hennessey (10)
Mercy Primary School

WITCHES HAVING FUN ON HALLOWE'EN

Witches on their broomsticks,
They're having so much fun,
They dance about and fly about,
They're having so much fun.
They go to catch children and
Use them for their spells.

But even witches sometimes get a fright
When the fireworks appear, banging at night.
Witches jump with fear and fright,
Nervously they stay out of sight.

Dawn Shannon (9)
Mercy Primary School

WINTER

There are more dark times than light
And I love to go out in the snow,
I like going out to play
And all the cars are driving slow.

I dress up really warm
For when I go out to play
In case there is a storm
Then I will run in my home.

I went for a walk
Around the Water Works
With my daddy and all we did was talk
While we were walking around.

When I went out in the fog
I was standing beside my pond
And I saw a frog
Then I went into the house.

It is really fun
In the winter,
I also like it in the sun
I really like it in all weathers.

Eimhear Meehan (9)
Mercy Primary School

TALKING

Talking, talking, talking,
We use it all the time.
Letters from the alphabet
Make good words sound just fine.

Talking is used all the time
In conversations, questions and answers too.
If we say words clearly,
Conversation can be easier for me and you.

This is how we make our friends
And hope are lives are enriched by them.
This is how we communicate,
Isn't it just great!

Maria Bannon (11)
Mercy Primary School

21ST CENTURY WORLD

For the millennium
I hope to see
A peaceful world for you and me.
Flying cars going far,
Animals safe in sea,
To work a car without a key.
No war,
Space travel, golf courses on the moon,
But most of all I want to see
A famous, rich, pretty me!

Fionnuala McGoldrick (10)
Mercy Primary School

WINTER

Long nights, short days,
Slippy roads, icy paths.
Children playing on their sleighs
Snow falls softly every day.

The days are getting cold and dull too
One thousand snowmen in every street.
I love snow do you?
Always sitting in front of your fire.

Having snow fights every day
All ponds turn into ice rings
And making snowmen that will stay up till May
Drinking hot drinks every day.

Clare-Louise Wilkinson (9)
Mercy Primary School

THE RIVER LAGAN

Reluctantly it passes,
Trickling on its way,
Swishing, swaying, bubbling,
Getting deeper as it plays.

The market town is crowded,
Men roaring for their goods,
The trickles of the river
Now sound like slushy foods.

Now we hear the ships
Floating on the sea,
Here no long a river,
The deepness is in me.

Colleen McIvor (11)
Mercy Primary School

The River Lagan

The long Lagan begins
As a trickle in Slieve Croob,
Up in the mountains
It's like a gentle pluck of a harp.
The river goes on and gets louder
It bubbles along
And has soon reached the market town of Dramore.
It whooshes on
To pass Lisburn, the linen industry.
The rushing river runs on
To gush past Central Station,
Where we can hear
The sounds of the train's engine.
It flows on
Like the sound of a rain stick
And reaches Belfast Harbour
Where the ship builders can be heard
Singing and whistling as they saunter home.
The river runs on
Gurgling as it goes,
Passing Albert Clock
We hear it chime
Six in the evening
Like the loud beat on the glockenspiel.
The River Lagan says its farewells
And we are welcomed by Belfast Lough.

Emma McCallan (11)
Mercy Primary School

THE LAGAN'S PATH

The Lagan starts as a stream,
Moving on swiftly,
Fulfilling a person's dream,
Growing in size,
Like the sound of a flute played softly.

Looking at the towpath,
From afar,
Children laughing cheerfully,
In the distance I see a car,
The sound of pizzicato played on a violin.

Past the old train station,
Past the Albert clock,
Going past the Waterfront Hall,
Down to the dock,
The sound of a drum beating hard.

Maria Maginness (11)
Mercy Primary School

SUNSHINE

When it is sunny I cool off by the sea
I collect up all the shells
And look at the sea to see what I can see
I love summer because I get tanned
And my little cousin says funny things like Wham.
I love to play with him especially when he says funny things,
I love summer, I love sunshine
I think nice things in summer
I love the colour of the sea
When the sun sparkles on me.

Joanne Rigby (9)
Mercy Primary School

THE RIVER LAGAN

As the river runs through Dromore
With ducks and swans on its back
Joining on to Lisburn's lake
It hears the whirl of spinning wheels
The headless horseman gallops on
The neigh of the horse as it is whipped
The clamp of its hooves as they hit the ground
The yell of *come on, come on!*
Echo through the trees
Men whistle as they do their work
The bell rings for break
At the Albert Clock rings for six o'clock
People scurry home for tea
As the river flows through the reeds
It gushes to a stop as joins the sea.

Sarah McKibbin (10)
Mercy Primary School

WHO AM I?

Starting as a trickle,
Dripping down the stones,
Passing through the market town
In the busy County Down.
The mooing of cows, the clucking of hens,
The screeching of people, writing with pens,
In past the busy and crowded Lisburn,
Clicking and whirring as spinning wheels turn,
Now on to Belfast and hear that noise,
The shouting and singing of young Irish boys.
Twisting and winding straight past me,
There goes the Lagan out to the sea.

Aoife Bradley (11)
Mercy Primary School

My Dreams

When I'm asleep
I can escape.
I can escape to the land of the dreams.
It's the only place,
I can get away from, or face,
My worries and fears, it seems.

I always have to get ready for dreamland.
The whole island is covered in sand.
Those are the good dreams,
Dreams at peace.
Bad dreams are always
Fighting at least.

But when I wake up,
This fantasy's gone
And next time I go to sleep,
I will dream on.

May Alexander (9)
Mercy Primary School

Kingfisher

The kingfisher dives,
Into the rippling stream,
She catches her minnow
And she gobbles it down,
Her bright coloured feathers,
Are a sight to see,
Warm chestnut orange,
Dazzling blue,
A little bit of white,
Just peeping through.

Nichola McBride (10)
Mercy Primary School

WIND

Wind moves clouds up in the sky,
Startles birds as they fly by
Wind moves heavy branches on trees,
Gives me goose bumps round my knees.

Wind dries washing on the line
And when there's a breeze it is fine,
To run and play and dance and shout
And knowing the Holy Spirit's about.

Winter time is coming near
And the bad winds are already here,
No more time for fun and play
Now the sun has gone away.

When at night I lie in bed
All sorts of things gather in my head,
All I hear is wind and rain,
Will I never see the sun again?

Rebecca Sheppard (10)
Mercy Primary School

THE BEAUTY OF CREATION

I like to watch the snow
And the way the wind blows,
See the birds in the sky
Hear the birds say hi!
Watch the hills go up and down
Oh God the world has never made a frown.
I watch the trees always sway
Thanks God for this day.

Nuala Mary McAllister (11)
Mercy Primary School

WINTER

Winter comes every day
Because we all want to play
We want it to blow and blow
And we want to play in the snow.

When I went to bed that night
I got a really terrible fright,
For there was stormy rain
I get scared again and again.

I like to play on winter days
Because it is so much fun
I like to throw big snowballs
Over my friends and everyone.

Deana Thompson (9)
Mercy Primary School

WINTER

Winter comes every year
Children all play in the snow
Snow fights are played every day
And everything goes OK.
My mummy and daddy are happy,
Because they can cuddle up close
But when I am in they never
Get to cuddle up close.
When my brother gets hit
He throws his snowballs away,
Then he says I hit myself on the head,
This very day.

Orlaigh McConnell (9)
Mercy Primary School

WINTER

In winter cars drive along icy roads
But when we get home the fire glows
In the middle of the day
Children really like to play.

We wear our gloves and coats
And most of the time
We do not sail on boats.

When I wake in the morning
I get dressed
And I go out and make a snowman.

I also go to bed
Covers up to my head
And dream the night away.

Lisa McAteer (9)
Mercy Primary School

FIREWORKS

Up it goes. *Bang*
It's sparkling bright,
The long rope is lit,
The sparks start to sizzle,
Sizzle, sizzle, whiz, whiz
Up they go flash,
Sparkle, sparkle, twinkle, twinkle,
Amazing lights,
It's so much fun
The firework display.

Rachelle Ward (9)
Mercy Primary School

WIND

Wind, wind, wind,
Twirling, swirling wind,
You can hear its mighty roar
But see nothing when you open the door.

Whistling, howling and roaring
Noises I hear when the wind is soaring
Papers flying all around
Lifting everything off the ground.

People wrap their clothes up tight
Against the wind with all its might
The wind that blows with all its force
Blow many a traveller off their course.

Caoimhe Britton (10)
Mercy Primary School

WINTER

In winter there are cold nights,
In winter the grounds are icy white
I like to sit close to the warm fire
And listen to exciting stories.

I like it when days are snowy white
To have lots of snowball fights,
Lots of cars drive slowly
There are also lots of shining lights.

There is thunder and lightning
Some frost as well,
I like it when the snow falls down and down,
In winter the days are often dull.

Caoimhe McGeough (9)
Mercy Primary School

THE KINGFISHER

Kingfisher, kingfisher,
Where do you fly?
High in the sky,
Flying like a jewel,
Soaring through the sky,
I see a fish.
I quickly dart down,
But I miss!
I patiently wait,
Until at last,
I catch a fish!
Higher and higher,
I soar through the sky!
A metallic blue flash
Dazzles the earth.

Sarah O'Donnell (10)
Mercy Primary School

TALKING

Voices, voices, everywhere,
Everyone making sounds,
I really love to talk
When my friends are all around
Chatting in the playground,
Gabbling on the phone
And I talk even more when I get home.

Emma Mowbray (10)
Mercy Primary School

THE BEAUTY OF CREATION

A poor women is very ill,
But very excited and still.
Her newborn baby has come at last,
Oh she is very glad!
This is spring time
And flowers are blooming,
Animals are born,
So this is a very special baby to her.
This is the beauty of creation,
I'm not surprised.
This is a big and beautiful world,
If we just open our eyes!

Sara Madden (11)
Mercy Primary School

THE SNOW CHILDREN

Feathery penguins everywhere,
Waiting for eggs to hatch,
Waiting, waiting, waiting.
Hoping the time comes soon.
Penguins will be chirping
Squabbling all together
Plump little tums,
Running all together
Hoping and jumping
Into the cold black sea.

Nicola Williams (10)
Mercy Primary School

A Viking Chant

Quick! Quick! Run and hide,
Hide your precious treasures now,
Beware, beware the Vikings are about,
They're fierce and mad,
They kill anyone in their way,
Their helmets made of iron,
Their shields are made of gold.
They'll grab and steal all your treasure,
They'll attack chiefs and churches
And holy sanctuaries,
Destroying monks' shrines and their books,
They attack with swords and axes,
Help! Help!
The terrified monks would say,
Save us from these demons.

Léontia McGrann (9)
Mercy Primary School

Christmas Morning

Jesus is born tonight,
Everybody is there in delight,
The baby is lying on hay,
Mary and Joseph knelt to pray.
Christmastime is here
The Millennium starts the new year,
Bringing lots of treats,
Celebrating 2000 on streets.

Laura Fusco (10)
Mercy Primary School

A Snow Poem

The snow falls on the ground,
All I want when the snow falls
Is a warm cup of tea.
I never take cold things like ice pops and
Coke because they are very cold.
When I go outside the snow is slushy
So I put on my wellies.

When the sun rises the snow
Begins to melt. All the muck
That is on the grass gets all
Over the bits that have no muck
And it destroys the grass.

Kelly Webb (9)
Mercy Primary School

A Viking Chant

The Vikings get ready for battle,
Their shields are silver and gold,
Hide all your treasures,
Lock up all your cares
They destroy homes
And make people unhappy,
They scream and shout,
They make our hearts sink fast,
Make the waves fierce and rough,
To make them less tough,
Oh! We are afraid of the Vikings.

Mariead McCann (10)
Mercy Primary School

WIND

Wind can be fierce, calm and mysterious,
It can be powerful and refreshing too,
You'll never know when it'll be coming,
It'll just pop up out of the blue.

Wind in a storm is very fierce,
Wind in a breeze is calm,
When wind blows gently on a dark, still night,
It can really frighten man.

Wind on a cold day freezes your toes,
Wind on a cold day freezes your nose,
Wind on a warm day cools you down,
Wind on a warm day refreshes you.

Wind is really very important,
It keeps us alive and well,
It keeps us awake on a long, boring day,
It really does help.

But we never know when it will come,
It will just pop up out of the blue,
But when it does come, just be grateful
For what it does and how it helps you.

Marcella Goudy (11)
Mercy Primary School

KINGFISHER

Perched on the branch,
Stood a kingfisher,
Waiting to catch a minnow,
With its metallic blue wings
And orange beast,
Kingfisher spots his dinner,
In goes kingfisher,
Catches his minnow,
Without a sound,
Then he soars into the sky,
Higher and higher into the clouds!

Grainne Gormley (10)
Mercy Primary School

THE IRON MAN

The Iron Man is made of metal
He eats things like stoves and kettles
He is about the size of a tall tree
But not as big as the blue foamy sea.
I hate the way he takes without asking
The towns people wished he was just passing
Outside he's made of very strong metal
But inside he's as soft as a petal.
When he moves you can only see his feet
The whole town are wishing the dragon he will defeat.

Danielle Quinn (11)
Mersey Street Primary School

The Commentator

Good morning and welcome to
Mersey Street Primary School,
Where we are watching
Miss Carson eagerly while
She is in our classroom
And the classroom looks in superb condition.
While Miss Carson the school teacher
Puts them on the attack,
She comes in the door
Is she, yes she closes the door.
She walks to her desk is she, is she
Yes, she lifts up a book
Then puts it back down.
Ooh! My word what is she doing?
She walks to her chair and sits down
And she gets up and goes to
Her desk, ooh I think she's crazy.
She gets the handkerchiefs
And goes and goes to the board
And she gets the board cleaner
And cleans the board.
Is this the end of this world?
I don't know!
My teacher is crazy, crazy!

Stephanie Bradley (10)
Mersey Street Primary School

Colours Of Day

White makes me think of a bride
White is Christmas time.
Yellow makes me feel happy
Yellow makes me think of sunshine.
Blue makes me sad and cold
Blue makes me think of Chelsea FC.
Red makes me think of blood and guts
Red makes me think of a lovely heart.
Black makes me feel scared and lonely
Black makes me think of darkness.

Michael Jackson (10)
Mersey Street Primary School

Chucked Out

They've stolen our home
but still no hope!
They still don't care
and the house is too much to pay!
But we keep on going and going.
We will cry,
We will lose our friends!
How will I survive
with no hope in the world!

Christopher Workman (11)
Mersey Street Primary School

FAMINE

F is for food there was very little of it,
A is for anger, of the poor people being evicted,
M is for the money they gave the landlords,
I is for I'm going to die.
N is for nothing to believe in.
E is for every day it is the same in my life.

Samuel Gray (11)
Mersey Street Primary School

THE RESULTS

Hooray, hooray,
It's finally the day,
The results are coming,
I pray to get an A.
Mum's making breakfast,
Dad's in Italy,
I'll call him on the cell-phone
He'll probably know it's me.
Running down the stairs,
After getting dressed so quick.
I see the postman coming
I'm so nervous, I feel sick,
Hooray, hooray,
It's finally the day
The results are coming
Please God I get an A.

Michaela Stewart (11)
Our Lady Of Lourdes School

HORSES

I hear a noise, can you hear it too?
The clip, clip, clop of a horse's shoe.
With a long stringy mane and a platted tail
Tucked up in his stable, away from the hail
As you jump on his saddle, to ride him around
His long swishy tail falls right down to the ground.
You feed him his oats in an outstretched palm
He moves not a muscle, but stays nice and calm
When he lies in his hay, munching his food
He acts quiet and friendly, like any horse should
He gallops about fields and hops over jumps
And if he falls over, he lands with a thump!
The power in his legs and strength in his back
As for might when he's running, well he doesn't lack!
And as you may know, they make a great mate
I've one more thing to say, horses are great!

Frances Caldwell (11)
Our Lady Of Lourdes School

THERE'S A MONSTER IN MY HOUSE!

There's a monster in my house
She's smelly, green and hairy
She smells like rotten eggs
And has 9 million legs
She's got 9 foot snakes for her hair
She hates me and I hate her
It's quite natural because she's a blister and
She's my sister!

Beth Mulhern (11)
Our Lady Of Lourdes School

MY DAD

My dad is a super dad,
He is sometimes serious and sometimes mad.
He thinks he's super fit,
But in the mornings he never gets out of his pit,
He cracks some jokes
But never smokes.
Some of his jokes are good
But some are rude,
He is quite smart
And good at art,
He goes from painting doors
To working in Dunnes Stores,
He likes cleaning his car
But would rather be in the bar.
At the weekend he likes to sit down
And act the clown,
At his leisure he likes to cook
Or read a funny book,
He likes to watch the football
And sometimes plays it in the hall,
He detests the plane
It puts him in pain
He would travel by boat or drive in the fast lane
But he absolutely hates the plane.
He lives his life to the full
Although he's middle aged, he thinks he's cool,
But my dad really is a super dad
Because he's never sad.

Aidan Small (11)
Our Lady Of Lourdes School

THE PLAYSTATION

A PlayStation is a boy's best friend
But I also have to recommend
The games people make are so much fun
If you don't believe me ask anyone
The magazines are great you see
They give cheats, solutions and codes
And they're a big hit around the globe.
More designers come every day
To make more games and get more pay.
When I grow up I want to be
A PlayStation designer, you will see.
The PlayStation world is full of joy
It's even better than the GameBoy
So for all you who have imagination
Go out right now and buy a PlayStation.

Richard McIlroy (11)
Our Lady Of Lourdes School

ALIENS

One day in space,
We will find an inhuman race,
They will come to conquer the Earth,
But will fail in the attempt,
They'll do as we once did,
Try to take over the Earth by a serious bid,
They'll try to blow up the Earth,
But they'll feel the wrath of the human race,
They'll wish they had gone to another place,
And now they've gone to carry on,
Or have they . . .

Fintan Maguire (11)
Our Lady Of Lourdes School

CREAKING FLOORBOARDS

11 o'clock I was reading in bed,
Dad came up the stairs and said,
'Come on, Claire, turn off the light,
It's nearly 12 o'clock midnight!
The midnight hour is meant for spooks
Not for children reading books!

I was reading a horror, gruesome and gory,
Not a relaxing bedtime story,
And in the dark odd thoughts came chasing
To set my throbbing heart a-racing.

Was that a footstep on the path?
A rustle at the garden shed?
Oh, go to sleep; stop worrying;
These things are simply in your head.

Help! I am absolutely certain
Something moved behind my curtain.
Now someone's creeping up the stairs,
This is the stuff of my nightmares!
Who's that scratching on the wall?
Is it a living thing at all?
Dive under the duvet, cover my ears,
Block the noises and calm my fears,
Eeek! The door swings open wide,
My scream somehow gets stuck inside.
'Oh please' I think, 'Don't get me yet,'
My duvet's gone, I'm in a sweat,
I bravely open up my eyes,
And almost faint with the surprise.
A scary demon?
Yep, you bet!
My baby sister Antoinette.

Claire Leonard (11)
Our Lady Of Lourdes School

MY BEST FRIEND

When I went into school
for the very first time
I saw a girl wearing
lemon and lime.

I said, 'Would you like
to be friends with me.'
And she said, 'Yes I would'
as sweet as can be.

As we grew older we
became better mates.
We went to each others
houses and played at the gates.

We went to the cinema
and went to the shop.
We even chatted on
the phone a lot.

If we get into a fight
we're mad but in our
hearts we're really
sad.

She is the bestest bud I say
and we are still best friends
today.

Clare Geier (11)
Our Lady Of Lourdes School

The Fox

The fox lay silently in his den,
Waiting for a careless wren.

Then he would jump and snap and kill,
When finished he'd be silent and still.

Movement! There the poor wren was
Having no fear of its predators paws.

Suddenly! Jump! Snap! Kill!
The little birds cry was horribly shrill.

Then the fox was still and silent,
For coming was the dreaded twilight.

And dreaded it was by all the prey,
They were sleeping through their predators day.

Perfect! A deer upon the hill,
Not a rustle, all is still.

Lunge! Slash! Like a blade!
The second kill that day was made.

Mark McCloskey (10)
Our Lady Of Lourdes School

Imaginations

Imaginations everywhere,
Some fly away with you in the air,
Some peoples are as big as a house,
Other peoples are as small as a louse.
Some peoples imaginations are very tall,
Others do not have any at all.

Mine ran away from me a while ago,
I tried my best but even though,
I could not find it, as hard as I tried,
I could not even see it, as hard as I spied.
A while later it returned quietly
But I could not imagine what happened to me.

James Parish (11)
Our Lady Of Lourdes School

MY DREAM STORE

Bags of jellies all around,
Sweets and drinks and food galore,
Bars of chocolate to add to that,
All in my dream store.

Teddy bears in bright coloured clothes,
CDs, books and loads more,
Pencils, crayons and felt-tip pens,
All in my dream store.

It's also got jumpers and trousers,
T-shirts, shorts and so much more,
Far better than school uniform,
All in my dream store.

And money is not a problem,
Nothing is too dear anymore,
There's no charge for anything, everything is free,
All in my dream store.

Claire Mulholland (11)
Our Lady Of Lourdes School

A Strange Night

Flying through the sky
It looks like a big apple pie.
It lands in the middle of France
Where they get out and start to dance.

They are round and small,
Do they bounce like a ball?
They have two square eyes
And wear ten yellow ties.

Their bodies are green
And they look very mean.
Their hair is blue
And curly too.

They shuffle along
While singing a song.
They went into a town
And walked up and down.

At the strange sight
In town that night
Some people stared
And others glared.

The aliens from Mars
Started driving other people's cars.
They drove all over town
And then knocked down a clown.

Some lights began to flash
So they began to dash.
So time to fly
Back to the sky.

Catriona Lawlor (11)
Our Lady Of Lourdes School

THE CLASS FROM HELL

The hell's angels they never stop
The teacher thinks her head will pop
For example Sean calls the class names
And Gerard plays his immature games.
Aidan cannot stop talking about football
Daniel won't stop getting into trouble at all.
Michael Hood can't ignore talking
Frances for jobs never stops walking
Smarty pants Claire gets everything right.
Jonathan shows off, getting into a fight.
Teresa comes in and only startin
Showing pictures of Ricky Martin.
As well as Eamon as good as gold
Is not like Conan, whose sometimes bold.

Colum Joseph McCrudden (11)
Our Lady Of Lourdes School

POKÉMON

Pikachu does a thunder jolt,
If he touches you he'll give you a bolt,
Bulbasaur's attacks including a tackle,
The only thing Psyduck does is waddle,
Charmander's flame-throwers really cool,
But compared to Charizard he's nothing but small,
Squirtle's attack is a water-gun,
But compared to Blastoise's hydropump it's just simply dumb,
Now that you've seen the world of Pokémon,
I hope you come back to have even more fun.

Eoghan Joseph Caldwell (10)
Our Lady Of Lourdes School

ANIMALS

Animals are amazing creatures
They have a lot of different features
The wolf has his teeth to attack his prey
While the horse in the stable says neigh.

The lion is fierce and strong
And the giraffe is elegant and long
The elephant has crinkly grey skin
And the rat loves to scavenge around in my bin.

The hyena with his eerie laugh
Is strong enough to eat a calf
The chimpanzee swings from tree to tree
And guess what he's just like me.

Michael Casement (11)
Our Lady Of Lourdes School

MY HAMSTER

My hamster is a lively thing,
He climbs up nearly everything.
He climbs up me, he climbs up Dad,
The hamster really does go mad.

When we let him on the floor
He tries to get through the door.
When he's in his cage again
He never rests, he goes insane.

If we put him in his ball
He tries to climb up the wall.
Then he realises he can't do it
So he has a massive fit.

Matthew Spence (10)
Rosetta Primary School

My Cat

When my cat sees a mouse
she chases it around the house.

When my cat drinks some milk
all her fur feels like silk.

When my cat goes to sleep,
the sound of a tin makes her peep.

When my cat eats her food
she is usually in a good mood.

When my cat falls to the floor
she usually lands on all fours.

When my cat kills a bird
her little stomach usually fills.

Dusty her name is, rhymes with what she is,
fussy I tell you, fussy she is.

James Chew (11)
Rosetta Primary School

My Meadow Dream

As I run through the feathery grass fields,
Droplets of rain land on my cheek.
The rainbow shines above me, colours from the sky.
The clouds so white, so fluffy.
They fall on the yellow grass and look like sheep grazing
On a beautiful spring day.
I feel that it's time to go.
As I walk back to reality, I wonder will I turn back?

Harriet Violet Cranston (10)
Rosetta Primary School

IN THE WOODLAND

At the crack of dawn
The birds start to sing
And the trees rustle
In the woodland.

The grey squirrel forages for nuts
And the dog chases the rabbits
While the swallows dance over the river
In the woodland.

A gunshot shatters the calmness.
It's hunters looking for game
But then the peace is restored
In the woodland.

Tawny owls fly silently
Looking for their next meal
While foxes and badgers hunt mice and voles
In the woodland.

Now that night has come
The cycle is complete
But it will start again tomorrow
In the woodland.

Graham Richardson (11)
Rosetta Primary School

SEPARATION

Separation is a gruelling thing,
Especially when you're young,
Put through hard and agonising times,
When your parents depart one another,
I felt I was being left.

Eventually they came back again,
But I had set my hopes too high,
My life suddenly went blank,
I guess I've got used to it,
Now it's been a year,
My life has changed dramatically
Since the separation.

James Bennett (11)
Rosetta Primary School

MAN UNITED

I was so tense and excited,
United versus Munich. What a game!
The match had begun,
The atmosphere was electric.
What a night it was going to be!

My nerves were exploding one by one,
Munich scored unfortunately,
I was absolutely destroyed.
The half was over with United still trailing a goal.

The second half had started.
I could not eat,
I was afraid to blink,
My eyes frozen to the screen.

Suddenly Sheringham scored.
I was jumping about with delight
And to top the night off Solskjaer scored.
The final whistle blew.
So United, the champions on the night
And I the happiest boy in the world.

Richard Burnett (10)
Rosetta Primary School

THE DAY THAT WE BROKE UP

The day that we broke up
Was the worst day of my life,
My parents didn't understand
How I felt that day.

The day that we broke up
Was such a terrible day,
I tried and tried to understand
Why he didn't love me.

The day that we broke up
I cried and cried for hours.
Why can't someone understand
About the day that we broke up?

Leanne Craig (10)
Rosetta Primary School

DREAMS OF FEAR

As I slept, the picture came into my mind.
The tall, dark figure, half-shaded by the darkness.
I took one step closer, then another.
The image slowly began to take shape.
It was fear trapped in the moment so lifelike yet so unreal.
Why was it there?
The coldness of it.
All the colour fled from my face.
I could see myself reflected.
An image of myself trapped in stone . . .
Transfixed with fear.
As I am in life.
Dreading the next dream.

Rebecca Gibson (11)
Rosetta Primary School

THE BIG MOMENT

Sitting out back
In the freezing cold
I start to tremble with nerves,
The excitement is setting in,
It's not far away now.

It's now within a minute.
Looking at the sky
We start to hear people in the city centre.
The countdown begins,
10, 9, 8, 7, 6, 5, 4, 3, 2, 1.

At last it is the new millennium,
The nerves fade away.
I'm happy it's passed without the world ending
As we go inside we wonder . . .
What it will be like in 1000 years.

Will our city be at peace?
Will fireworks rend the sky?
Will my descendants sit as I have done
Watching a Belfast, night sky?

Philip Todd (10)
Rosetta Primary School

HALLOWE'EN FIREWORKS

Fireworks whiz and fizz,
Squeal and bang.
Reflecting on the river, orange red and blue.
Gigantic fountain in the air like a bullet.
Little children shudder and jump.
But soon the sky is velvet black again.

Peter Davison (10)
Rosetta Primary School

THE RESULTS

It was the day I had been waiting for.

I had long awaited this very day
Through the door came the letter
It thudded to the floor with a dead beat.

We were all nervous, especially me
I was agitated, my hands shook
A sheen of sweat covered my brow.
My mum opened the envelope and
                    pulled out a letter.
She read it.
I'd got a 'C'
I'd passed the test that frightened me,
But although the future frightens me
This was the best day of my life.

Paul Dougan (11)
Rosetta Primary School

VALENTINES DAY

It's Valentines Day,
The day I fell in love.
She was adorable.
I sent her a card,
I even sent her a necklace and a bobble,
But she didn't really love me.
I asked the teacher for my necklace back
because I thought she put it in the bin
but she didn't.
I still want her,
Even if she doesn't care.

Andrew McElroy (10)
Rosetta Primary School

FIRE

Fire burns with red and orange.
Fire spreads with heat and flames.
Fire destroys houses and buildings.
Fire burns wooden sticks and canes.

Fire feeds on gas and air,
Both together make a nasty pair.
Put together with such might,
Put up such a dangerous fight.

Now the fire is burning up,
Destroying everything in its way.
Oh no, here it's coming,
Come let's run away.

Now the fire is almost out . . .
The flame is burning away . . .
The fire is dead.

Dougal Crawford (10)
Rosetta Primary School

WALKING THROUGH THE WOODS

Waterfalls fall splashing, bashing with fury and force,
Then trickle downstream, gently, all anger gone,
Under the bridge, around the black, dull rocks.
I see some fish swimming gracefully through trapped air bubbles.
The still, shimmering waters,
The silky sky, swathed in mist,
Gives an air of mystery to my woods.

Nicole Allen (10)
Rosetta Primary School

MY FREDDIE

My Freddie
Is a beautiful, five year old bird.
He flaps his wings in a bare room.

He sits on my shoulder watching TV.
If Freddie died I would feel lost,
I would bury him in my back garden.

He is my best friend
With his white and yellow and orange sideburns.
I love my little friend.

I wish I didn't have to keep him in a cage
But if I gave him freedom
I would lose him
And be lost myself.

Andrew Swain (11)
Rosetta Primary School

END OF A LIFE

Coloured cascades of leaves fall from them.
Sparkling white silk rests on them.
The golden sun shines on them.
Then all at once developers chop their bright green leaves.
Their long sprawling hands.
Their crusty brown bark.
My heart dies with the once beautiful tree.

Ruth Jennings (11)
Rosetta Primary School

LOVE

Love is what makes life worth living.
Makes a happy feeling inside.
It gets the heart pounding.
Love is what makes life worth living.

Loves makes the world go round.
It's our friends and families, old and young.
The feeling is enjoyment.
Love makes the world go round.

What would the world be without it?
Sad and lonely probably.
Our life would be soulless.
What would the world be without love?

Daniel Stewart (11)
Rosetta Primary School

SHADOWS

I feel a shiver up my spine as I see the shadow
creeping across the wall.
I watch with fear as the shadow creeps into my bedroom.
I stand still, quivering at the thought.
Then, slowly I walk into my room to find my brother crying,
All colour drained from his face.
I know that someone or something has scared him . . .
Maybe the stories are true about my house and its troubled past.
Can shadows hurt me
Or just the fear . . .?

Kathy Reid (10)
Rosetta Primary School

BYE-BYE GREAT GRANNY!

My great granny died when I was just seven
And my daddy said she floated up to Heaven.
I was really sad that she was dead,
So may God rest her little head.

So Great Granny if you are up there
Please listen to my little prayer.

Dear Granny,
         I hope you are keeping well
And you are looking after yourself.
I just want to let you know that I miss you.
I love you and I hope you are keeping well.
The time has come for me to go. Talk to you soon.
               Bye-bye Granny.
                  Amen.

Lesley Jordan (10)
Rosetta Primary School

MY GRANNY

My granny is my life,
She is the most affectionate person I know.
We all long for someone like her.
I spend my afternoons with her,
Stopping loneliness from killing her, killing me.
I dread to think of when she dies,
My whole life will be over.
Everything I had,
Everything I've done
Will all die with her.
I will be alone, bereft of her love.

Rebecca Sleator (11)
Rosetta Primary School

DRUGS

Drugs are dangerous, they are a crime,
For a while they make you feel fine.

They come in all different sizes and shapes,
After a while you'll feel as if you want to escape.

The terrible feeling they give you deep down
Take it from the experts, don't act as a clown.

Drugs are a killer, they'll make you fly high,
Way up there in heaven, up in the sky.

So now you know that drugs can kill,
If you're thinking of taking them, start writing your will.

Jennifer Smyth (10)
Rosetta Primary School

MY BABY SISTER

The day my sister was born
I was happy.
I held her.
She had bright blue eyes
And fuzzy hair.
When I first held her she was sleeping,
Tiny little ears peeking out,
Long fingers gripped mine,
She felt light and warm.
I smelt her smell of talc and milk
And I knew that I would love her forever.

Karen Oliver (10)
Rosetta Primary School

STATUE

In the middle of the park,
There sits the big stone man
Constantly watching the great oak tree,
Listening to the robin's song.

He sits and sees
My friend chasing me,
Round and round him we run,
The wind whistling in my hair.

When night falls
And all is quiet,
Still he sits there,
The big stone man.

Sarah McKee (11)
Rosetta Primary School

FOOTBALL

Football is the season,
The ball is black and white.
When you score a goal
Your face fills with delight.

When you score a goal the fans go mad,
Some of the peelers have barriers in their hands.
Managers are rioting with the patrol
But no - the players did not score.

It's near the end of the match,
The referee is checking his watch,
The players have nearly scored,
No, the final whistle has blown.

Thomas McGowan (11)
Rosetta Primary School

NIGHTMARE

I have just had a nightmare
But I am not sure what is was about.
I think it was a voice,
It was an evil voice
Saying nasty and wicked things.

I think in my nightmare
I could see drips of blood from the ceiling.
The drips hit the ground and made puddles,
The puddles turned into a flood of blood.

The flood turned into a swimming pool.
I tried to get out.
Then a bony hand came out of the blood
And grabbed me.

Joe Shearer (11)
Rosetta Primary School

THE SNOWMAN

Winter is here, the snow is falling,
I can hear my friends all calling,
'Shantelle, Shantelle come out to play,
Let's all build a snowman today.'

We build a big snowman and call him Jack.
We give him eyes, a nose and a hat.
Winter is coming close to an end,
We are getting closer to losing a friend.

Jack is melting more each day and
Then one day he just went away.
Spring is now on its way.

Shantelle O'Kane (8)
St Anthony's Primary School

Autumn

Autumn is a happy time.
The birds like to sing and chirp.
The green leaves fall from the trees.
I love the colours of autumn leaves,
Yellow, red, green, orange and brown.
Watch as the leaves tumble down.
It is cold and breezy in autumn time,
The wind blows my hair into my eyes.
I do not like going out at night,
It is very dull and not so bright.
I hear the sounds, snap, crackle and crunch under feet.
The season of autumn really is a treat.
'Wrap up warm,' my mum calls.
Jack Frost will soon be here.
Autumn will eventually disappear
As winter now creeps in.

Sami-Jo lavery (9)
St Anthony's Primary School

The Howling, Whistling Wind

As the howling, whistling wind
Blows through the streets,
Children play with their paper planes
As the water butt leaks.

People's washing out on the line
While they drink up their rosy red wine.
Birds looking at the chicks in the nest,
Watching, watching as they have a good rest.

As the wind puffs up its cheeks and blows
Newborn babies twinkle their toes.
And as the black cat looks at the sky,
Wishing, wishing that it would be dry.

Gary Ferguson (11)
St Anthony's Primary School

WIND

The wind howled and
molested the trees.
hardened features.
As I was sitting
watching out the back
window in my house.
Swoosh, swoosh
the wind was struggling
but this old tree had
stood for many years
and wasn't going to give up
that easily.
The wind
made the tree struggle.
Now the wind
was intense, *whoosh.*
Whoosh, gale force
winds at 70mph.
Bang, bang, clatter.
The tree lived to
fight another day.

Rory O'Hanlon (10)
St Anthony's Primary School

WINTER

Once I had a snowman, he was very tall,
In fact he was taller than the garden wall.
The snow began to melt
And my snowman got very small.

The winter days got cold and dark
So I could not get to the park.
I had to sit at home all day
And wish that I could get out to play.

The flowers did not bloom
And you didn't see much of the moon.
The sun started to come out
And my snowman was not about.

The winter days got cold and breezy
And I started to get sneezy.
I sat at home all day and cried,
I wished that I had tried to build
My snowman once again before spring
Would come and my efforts would be in vain.

Seana Rooney (9)
St Anthony's Primary School

MY PONY

My pony goes munch, munch, munch.
It's just so cute and brown.
I ride on it all day
And sometimes trot into town.
It goes so fast and wriggly
that when I get off I am really dizzy.

One day she fell and broke
her knee and went to the vet.
When she got better
I was so happy because she is my pet.
I gave her food,
Her favourite one,
A crunchy, crumbly chocolate bun.

Orla Campbell (8)
St Bride's Primary School

JACK FROST

Jack Frost is about
So beware, don't go out
He will give you a chill
I tell you, he will!

Jack Frost is outside,
Oh no!
Let's go and hide.

Oh no!
We have to go out,
The dog is gone!
Oh do come on!

It is very cold
As Mum told,
Jack Frost has got me!

He has put me in
A pot of ice,
I can tell!

Maria Cushinan (9)
St Bride's Primary School

THE COLOURS OF THE NIGHT

The colours of the night are very beautiful,
Inky black, dusky brown,
There are a lot more you know.
Let's find them out.
Deep purple, sapphire blue,
The stars are so bright in the night,
Oh they are so beautiful.

At night the owls hoot.
At night the werewolves howl
At night the cats run about.
In the nice bright morning
The milkman comes rattling by.

Conor Heaney (8)
St Bride's Primary School

ONE DARK HALLOWE'EN DREAM

One inky black Hallowe'en night
All the costumes and masks gave me a fright.
I went out to 'trick or treat',
What kind of people did I meet?
You wouldn't believe what they gave,
One lived in a spooky cave.
They all ganged up on me,
Who were they, she or he?
But my mum woke me up to see
Thank goodness it was only a dream
And I didn't have to scream!

Jeri Smith Cronin (8)
St Bride's Primary School

School Is Cool

I go to school each day,
To see my friends and
Work and play.
School is cool.

I go to school each day,
On the school bus,
It saves a lot of fuss.
School is cool.

I go to school each day,
Wearing my uniform,
It is grey.
School is cool.

At 3 o'clock each day,
I go home,
Bye friends I'm off to play but,
School is cool!

Niamh Doyle (9)
St Bride's Primary School

My Fat Cat

My fluffy cat is rather fat.
He loves to chase a slippery rat.
He is quite small, he isn't tall.
His favourite toy is a silver ball.
He goes out in the midnight moon
And soon he will be six.
I love my golden tiger cat
Who gets up to many tricks.

Orla Cassidy (8)
St Bride's Primary School

My Horrible Sister

My sister is really ugly,
She isn't very nice.
Her favourite animals in the world
are yucky, poisonous mice.

Her boyfriend is wicked,
He is very cruel,
He always goes to the toilet
in our swimming pool,
Her favourite food is sweetcorn,
She likes it very much.
I hardly understand her
because she speaks in Dutch.

Luke McCann (8)
St Bride's Primary School

The Frosty Man

When I step up to him he growls,
Then I start to have a howl.
I am scared in my head.
I don't know what to say,
I'll just have to get out of his way.
He has a snow body like a piece of salami.
I am innocent, I would not do any harm.
I will eat you if I can.
I quickly got out of the way
And that is it for another day.

Ronan O'Kane (8)
St Bride's Primary School

THE WEE WHITE BUNNY

One stormy winter's night
A little bunny came into sight.
It was fluffy and all white,
The sky was black, it was night.

I took it in and gave it food,
When it woke up it was good.
It did not bounce all around
It just lay there on the ground.

Then it saw me standing there,
It jumped up into the air
And then sat up and began to stare.

Rebecca Copeland (8)
St Bride's Primary School

STARS

One dark, dark night
The stars came out,
And one came down on me,
I took it inside,
And I hid it inside,
And it glittered through the night.
The stars are bright to brighten
up the night and keep an eye on me.

Aoife Campbell (8)
St Bride's Primary School

WINTER POEM

Winter is coming, winter is cold.
Snow and sleet makes your nose cold.
But there are some good things about snow,
You can make snowmen, and best of all have snowball fights.
But remember to put on warm clothes or your nose will be sore,
                                              cold and red and pink.
And worst of all you might catch a cold with coughs and sneezes.
And if you don't have any warm clothes,
I think you would best stay inside, and keep warm!

Andrew Gribben (8)
St Bride's Primary School

TIGGER

I have a little kitten
That loves up-high sittin'.
Her name is Tigger
And each day gets bigger and bigger.

She has a sticky out claw
On her front left paw.
Her coat is browny black
Especially on her back.
It's butter she likes lickin'
But best of all loves chicken!

Maeve McGourty (9)
St Bride's Primary School

HOT AIR BALLOONS

Up, up and away
Sailing high in the sky
A colourful balloon filled with hot air
Taking me way up high!

Up, up and away
Over the mountain tops,
I am having so much fun
I wish this ride would never stop!

Up, up and away
I've been on this ride forever.
This balloon will never land
Never, never, never!

Catherine Loughrey (8)
St Bride's Primary School

WINTER WEATHER

The weather is bad,
And snow is deep,
And as Jack Frost comes,
Winter really starts to come.
It is cold at night,
And wet in day,
As Jack Frost gets his way.
The weather is cold,
As the snow falls,
We huddle up,
As it is cold.

Jamie Lavery (8)
St Bride's Primary School

Rascal

Rascal is a playful
Dog
He really lives up
To his name.

When I come home
He jumps
Up and down
Like a sweet little pup.

He is a yucky dog
But my kind
Of yucky
Dog.

When he goes
For a walk
He tugs and pulls
With all his might.

When he's asleep
You would
Have said he
Was a little angel.

Hannah McKnight (9)
St Bride's Primary School

JACK FROST

Jack Frost is in the garden.
Hopping around having fun,
And doing his job.

Jack Frost is in the garden.
Looking for mischief all around and
Having lots of luck and fun.

Jack Frost is in the garden
Now that I am out I will
Try and catch him.

Jack Frost is in the garden.
I haven't caught him for he's
Freezing our fingers and toes.

Hannah McGrath (8)
St Bride's Primary School

WINTER IS HERE

Winter is here the trees are bare the animals
Hibernate and the birds migrate. The robin
Waiting at your doorstep looking for his food
Winter is here!

The days get shorter the nights get longer
Because winter is here. The boys and girls are
Making snowmen and having snowball fights
Winter is here!

Carl Fitzpatrick (9)
St Bride's Primary School

HIBERNATION

The squirrels hibernate in winter,
They go to sleep in trees they gather,
Fruit and nuts and sleep all through,
the cold winter when the snow falls,
The rabbits also go to sleep in wintertime.
They dig burrows in the ground,
And go to sleep in wintertime,
And they wake up in springtime.
The badger and the mole go to
sleep in the wintertime.
They go to sleep under the ground as well as,
The rabbits, the moles go deeper than the
badgers in winter.

Conor McGuigan
St Bride's Primary School

PETS

I feed my dog every day
I've got a cat, now think of that.
I think my rabbit is cute as can be,
And then there's my parrot who follows me.

My fox's name is Box
Because he likes to sit
And I really think he's crazy
Because he sits on a box full of socks!

I have a hen called Clucky
And a bird that's always mucky
Then there's a hare called Lucky
And that's the whole family!

Hannah Smyth (8)
St Bride's Primary School

She is so full of life and fun
I show her off to everyone
She smiles at them and looks so shy
But I see the twinkle in her eye.

No more days bored and alone
Since my little sister came into our home.

Sinead McCourt (9)
St Mary's Star Of The Sea, Primary School

PLEASE SIR, PLEASE MISS

Please Sir it's time for dinner,
I want to be first to be the winner.

Please Miss I was late,
I couldn't open the garden gate.

Please Sir, can I go out to play
For it is a sunny day?

Please Miss the flowers are dead.
Maybe they're asleep, maybe they're in bed.

Please Sir there are cards for you,
Just to say, 'How do you do.'

Please Miss the leaves are brown,
The wind has blown them down to the ground.

Shauna McAleenan (8)
St Mary's Star Of The Sea, Primary School

MILLENNIUM

What does the millennium have in store
Robots, computers and automatic doors
Silver space-age outfits are what we'll wear soon,
Goldfish bowl helmets and holidays on the Moon.
Millennium Dome, Millennium Wheel, what will we do
                                        after the millennium?
Will we still act crazy or just plain lazy because
We'll have a robot slave to clear up after us?
Will we have a car or catch a bus,
To go to work and stuff?
I wonder will we go to work at all?
All these questions in my head,
I'd rather have the answers instead.

Shauna McGuiness (10)
St Mary's Star Of The Sea, Primary School

ELEVEN PLUS RESULTS

I went downstairs
Nothing was there
I waited a while to see what was there.
A knock on the door which gave me a scare
But it was just my grandma.
Then something came through the letter box
But it was my mummy's new silver watch.
Get on your coat, get in the car
And we'll know your results within the hour.
I found a letter which said Miss Stephanie Hall
I opened it and gave a ball.
'Yes' I passed it all.

Stephanie Hall (10)
St Mary's Star Of The Sea, Primary School

SCHOOL SWEET SCHOOL

In school I like to run about and play,
Enjoy myself and have a wonderful day.
As for my friends, they hate school.
They don't like playing with sand till our buckets are full.

When I say, I like school, all my friends go, 'Po!'
What's wrong with school, I like it, don't you?
They all don't like school and try to get out
But if they try this, '100 lines' is what my teacher will shout.

My favourite subjects are English and maths,
But all my friends would rather eat a taz.
When they're out playing I'd rather do work
But if I did this they'd call me a jerk.

People love it when the bell goes,
They're in such a hurry, they stand on my toes.
They also love it when they can eat Monster Munch,
And sandwiches and other things for lunch.

Everyone in my class, including my mate
Doesn't like school I mean hate.
Most people like going home sick and boking
Is this all true, or am I joking.

Colleen McLaughlin (10)
St Mary's Star Of The Sea, Primary School

MILLENNIUM WRONGS

The bug was set to strike,
At twelve o'clock of the night.
The new-age dawned,
It didn't!

Nostradamus predicted the world,
Would end as soon as the calendars became 00!
It didn't!

They said what they thought,
But they were way wrong.
Computers are going,
The world is still here!
They were all wrong!

Matthew McIlveen (10)
St Mary's Star Of The Sea, Primary School

A MILLENNIUM FEAR

The bug is coming,
Quick everyone hide.
What's that noise?
I feel all funny inside.
I'm confused,
What's the date?
I've lost all my memory,
Oh no I'm too late.
The bug has got me!
That wretched little thing,
I'm scared!
He might take over the world and become king!

Paul O'Neill (10)
St Mary's Star Of The Sea, Primary School

DOCTORS, DOCTORS

Doctors, doctors
Knock on the door.
With little suitcases
Which lay on floors.

They have injections
Which they stick into you
And medicines,
Which taste very funny.

Bandages and plasters,
Which cure broken arms.
Tablets taste sour
Some which are shaped big and hard.

Christopher Patterson (11)
St Mary's Star Of The Sea, Primary School

SUMMER

Summer, summer, summer's here
It's my favourite time of year.
Now we can go out and play
No more school hip, hip hooray.

Summer's here, summer's there, summer's everywhere.
There's more fun and more fun
There's no homework to be done.

Kathryn Reynolds (10)
St Mary's Star Of The Sea, Primary School

SUMMER

S ummer has lots of sunny days.
U mbrellas are put away.
M orning sky has a wonderful glow
M idsummer nights we stay at home
E veryone strolls along so slow
R oaring by are cars with nowhere to go.

Deborah Reynolds (8)
St Mary's Star Of The Sea, Primary School

OUR CAR

I love our car,
It takes me everywhere near and far.
It takes us to the shops and school,
It also takes us to the swimming pool.
A car saves us from getting the bus,
It saves us from a lot of fuss.
The car is very fast,
So it doesn't make our journey last.

Michael Kane (8)
St Mary's Star Of The Sea, Primary School

SPRING

Spring is joyful happy and bright,
The sun is still up when it is night.
The flowers pop up to say hello
And say goodbye to the worms below.
The animals wake up from their long, long sleep,
And the birds give a welcoming cheep.

Kerrie O'Hanlon (8)
St Mary's Star Of The Sea, Primary School

WONDERFUL WET WEATHER

The heavy rain falls down like sharp razor blades,
All the sad people with heavy sandbags at their doors.
My couch went out the door,
I got a speeding ticket for doing 35 mph
My school is cancelled; what a relief!
Now I can stay in bed and rest my very sore head.
I feel great 'cause now I can stay up late,
My mummy is very sad 'cause school is flooded.
Our rusty old gutter round the side,
Has fallen down and died!
Lots of multicoloured umbrellas walking
                             down the street,
I can't get to sleep at night because
      we have some more torrential rain!

Daniel Hughes (11)
St Mary's Star Of The Sea, Primary School

THIS IS THE NIGHT

This is the night when witches cast spells,
When dead wake up and fall into wells.
This is the night when ghosts go boo!
When vampires drink blood and are scary too.

This is the night when mummies are out,
When zombies wake and walk about.
This is the night when you have fun,
When you dress up and get sweets and buns.

Gerard McLaughlin (11)
St Mary's Star Of The Sea, Primary School

HALLOWE'EN POEM

In a graveyard one dark night,
Everyone got a terrible fright.
A witch jumped out with a crooked nose,
And started changing everyone's toes.

The very next night the witch got a fright,
Instead of changing everyone's toes,
She changed her own nose.
She tried to change it back,
But nearly broke her own back.

Stephanie Murtagh (11)
St Mary's Star Of The Sea, Primary School

AUTUMN

Autumn leaves turn golden brown
All red squirrels dance around
Hedgehogs always hibernate resting peaceful
All the blackbirds sing with their mates
Always printing things to date
Let's all pick some acorns
Let's all play in leaves
Autumn is so beautiful
Let's all swing in trees.

Eamonn Privilege (7)
St Mary's Star Of The Sea, Primary School

SNOW

One winter's day I made a snowman
As pretty as could be.
My brother threw some snowballs
and our snowman fell right down.
Our snowman was made from snow
With a carrot for his nose,
then buttons for his tummy,
and then the snowman was perfect as can be.
My little mate sat in the garden all day long.
When the sun came out my little snowman well,
He melted down.

Ellen Toner (8)
St Bride's Primary School

MY FAVOURITE TEAM

Man United are my team
When they play it's like a dream.
My favourite player is Paul Scholes
That's because he scores great goals.
I like to watch them on TV
They'll score one goal or maybe three.
I always hope that they will win
And when they do I like to grin.
I love it when Beckham makes a pass
The ball flies straight across the grass.
Big Jaap Stam is very tall
And when he plays he's like a wall.
Man United aren't like the rest
That's because they are the best.

Stephen Logan (10)
St Mary's Star Of The Sea, Primary School

Wonderful Wet Weather

Rain coming down so hard,
All those puddles in my yard.
Parents calling their children in.
I heard someone say the rain is such a sin.
I wonder if the poor little insects are still alive,
I know all the bees will be in a hive.
I wonder why the rain comes this day.
I wonder what it would be like on the sandy bay.
Although this day is very wet,
Some people will make a bet.
Some day the rain will stop
And the sun will come over the top.
Umbrellas dancing about,
Until the sun comes out.
I'm actually glad this wet rain has come,
Because look at how much poetry I have got done.

Joanne Craven (11)
St Mary's Star Of The Sea, Primary School

Spring

S pring is when the flowers grow buds,
P eople plant beautiful flowers in spring.
R oses are very pretty at this time of year.
I n the house nobody's there, all out doing something fun.
N ew leaves starting to appear on trees.
G ardeners start to plant seeds of all different flowers.

Anthony Kelly (9)
St Mary's Star Of The Sea, Primary School

MY DOG

I have a dog big and strong,
Who loves to play all day long.
With a tail so long and thick,
He enjoys running for a stick.

I take him for his daily walk,
I love to watch his face when I talk.
He jumps and jumps with joy,
When I tell him, 'What a good boy!'

When we pass the river, he loves to splash,
Into the water he goes with a dash.
Throwing a stone for him to play,
Makes for a very enjoyable day.

On his lead and heading for home,
He still wants to run and roam.
I hold him tight and pat his head
And tell him he'll soon be fed.

With him walking by my side,
People try to run and hide.
'Cause he is large, big and wide,
I walk him mostly on the tide.

On wet days inside we stay,
Sitting at the fire and having a play.
Hoping for tomorrow and a better day,
So we can enjoy our walk and fun in the hay.

I love my dog with all my heart,
I hope we will never have to part.
To not have my faithful friend
Would drive me around the bend.

Mark Magee (10)
St Mary's Star Of The Sea, Primary School

CATS

Cats are my favourite animals
Cuddly, cute and sweet
Crawling here and there
A ball of fluff when sitting down
In the street and in the town
Climbing all around.

Jumping, purring. chasing mice
Get on their wrong side and cats aren't nice.
Eating, drinking, running fast,
A ball of fluff just sprinting past.
Cats are made to last.

Lipping, lapping from their bowl
Cats are good not bold.
If I were a cat I would purr and purr
Get all the humans to stroke my fur.
Cats need all the proper care.

Cats are brilliant, cats are nice
Running, jumping, eating mice.
Long swishing tail and big sharp claws
Little tiny ears and sweet little paws.

Cats are just the best thing out
They make no noise all about.
So now we've got it, cats are good
Lipping, lapping up their food.

Justin McReynolds (10)
St Mary's Star Of The Sea, Primary School

AUTUMN

It's Mother Nature's time again,
To brighten up the lane.
With gold and crimson and yellow,
Because it's autumn once again.
The toadstool wood is golden,
As is the big oak tree.
The leaves are crinkly and mottled
And the wind makes you feel free.
The sun is breaking through the clouds
And insects are gathered in crowds.
The weeping willow is yellow,
It looks like a golden waterfall.
My garden is an autumn valley,
On this autumn eve.

Deaglan Privilege (10)
St Mary's Star Of The Sea, Primary School

LIFE

Life is all around us no matter where we look,
You never know it could be even in a book.
Life as I say is in a plant, in a sweet.
And everyone knows it's even in the street.

Life is you and I.
There's life in a pie.
There's life inside the Earth.
There's life up in the air, so no matter where you look
You always see life, so even if you try,
You'll be there for quite a while.

Mary-Anna Clarke (9)
St Mary's Star Of The Sea, Primary School

WHY AND HOW?

Why does a dog bark
I'd like to know
And why it rains or why it's sunny
Or even why does it snow?

Could nobody answer this question
Some answers yet untold
Piles and piles of questions
Each minute another one unfolds.

How did the moon form
And how do good people become bad?
It is a bit strange.
How do and why do people cry when they are sad?

Could nobody answer this question?
Some answers yet untold
Piles and piles of questions
Each minute another one unfolds.

Scientists know these answers
But they are not sure
Like doctors and nurses
Are not sure about a medicine or a cure.
How did we get here?
Was it God and his magic
That made us appear?

Still other questions remain
And another day passes
You'll never know if it could be the same.

Ashlene Flynn (10)
St Mary's Star Of The Sea, Primary School

WONDERFUL WET WEATHER

I am in the house,
It's as quiet as a mouse.
The rain is coming down torrentially,
The gutters are overflowing.
All the lights are glowing,
Because it's so dark.
Coloured umbrellas walking in the park!

We've sandbags under the door.
So the water doesn't come in,
People floating down the road 'cause they're so poor.
Car wipers can't keep up with the lashing rain,
People shouting 'cause they're in pain.
I dare to think next will be us.
I hope it'll be over just after dusk.

Some water is coming in now.
We're gonners now, we're gonners.
But the funny bit is.
The cows coming down on a boat,
They're mooing away wondering what's happened.
They probably think someone's left the tap on,
The rain lashing down and the place flooded.

Splashing school kids on the road,
People running with their load.
Lots of power cuts,
Lots of wrecked tree huts.
Gallons of water,
Coming through the gutter.
I can't sleep because the rain's
      tapping on my window.

Ciara Rooney (11)
St Mary's Star Of The Sea, Primary School

MY NAUGHTY LITTLE SISTER

My naughty little sister
Oh how I love her so.
She never seems to sleep at all
It's always go, go, go.

My bedroom that was once so neat
Is now a mess of chews and sweets
Books here, clothes there
Such a mess everywhere!

Perfume bottles are no longer full
Lipstick painted on the wall.
Earrings scattered on the floor
Cartoons scribbled on my door.

A toy box sits alone and bare
Once a lot of toys lived there.
The books that once stood tall and neat
Are scattered all about my feet.

The bathroom too that was so fresh,
Is now another awful mess.
A toothpaste tube no longer full
She thinks the bath is a swimming pool.

The kitchen has escaped her touch
She doesn't seem to like it much.
My mum has taken lots of care
To make sure she doesn't wander there.